AFRICA SOLO

AFRICA SOLO

A JOURNEY ACROSS THE SAHARA, SAHEL, AND CONGO

KEVIN KERTSCHER

STEERFORTH PRESS
SOUTH ROYALTON, VERMONT

For information about permission to reproduce
selections from this book, write to:
Steerforth Press L.C., P.O. Box 70, South Royalton, Vermont 05068.

Library of Congress Cataloging-in-Publication Data
Kertscher, Kevin, 1964-
Africa solo : a journey across the Sahara, Sahel, and Congo / Kevin Kertscher
p. cm.
ISBN 1-883642-94-9 (alk. paper)
1. Sahel—Description and travel. 2. Sahara—Description
and travel. 3. Congo—Description and travel.
4. Kertscher, Kevin, 1964-   —Journes—Africa.   I. Title.
DT528.K39   1998
916.6—dc21   97-47401
                                            CIP

ISBN 1-883642-94-9

The text of this book was composed by Steerforth Press
using a digital version of Goudy.

Manufactured in the United States of America

FIRST EDITION

For my Great Aunt, Winefred Evans;
And my sweethearts, Kate and Haley.

CONTENTS

Maps & Illustrations   ix

THE SAHARA

Stepping Off   5
Solitude   14
Close Call   22
Golden Rule of the Desert   33
Desert Fever   41
The Leader, The Mechanic, The Cook,
   and the American   47

THE SAHEL

Frontier Banquet   67
Change of Pace   75
The Heart of West Africa   82
The Big Village   89
New Country   95
Comfortable Dates   101
A Long Way From Home   109
Quiet Time   116
A Little Sightseeing   125
Priorities   132
Mad Dash   137

THE CONGO

Soldiers' Playground   153
Another World   158
River of Stars   166
Congo Boat   170
Into the Jungle   182
Starting Over   196

SANCTUARY

Across the Equator   217
Gorilla Highlands   221
Out in the Open   232
Flying Away   244

Afterword   253

Acknowledgements   257

MAPS

Africa x-xi
The Sahara Region 3
The Sahel Region 65
Central Africa 151
East Africa 215

PHOTOGRAPHS

Negotiating loose sand south of
  In Salah in the Algerian Sahara 1

Fishing from a pirogue on the
  Niger River in Mali 63

Waiting for barges to be reconnected
  on the Congo River 149

A baby mountain gorilla in the
  Virunga National Park, East Africa 213

On the banks of the Mongala River,
  Democratic Republic of the Congo 251

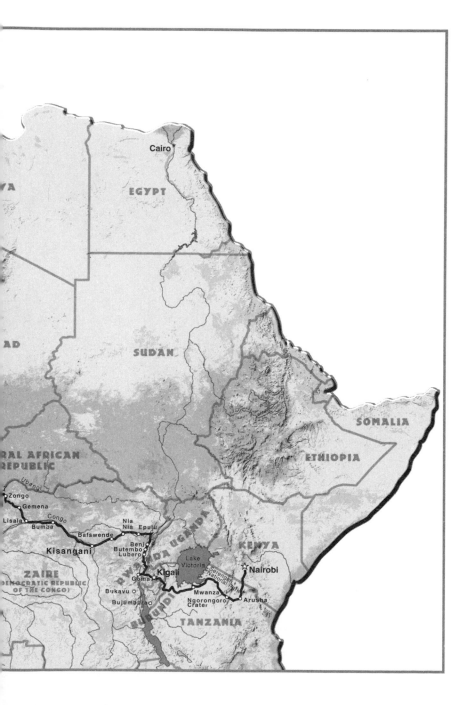

The artist appeals to that part of our being which is not dependent on wisdom. . . . He speaks to our capacity for delight and wonder, to the sense of mystery surrounding our lives: to our sense of pity, and beauty, and pain.

JOSEPH CONRAD

THE SAHARA

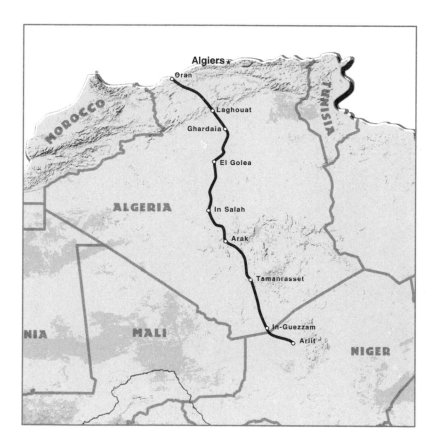

*He who does not travel does not know
the value of men. Therefore wander!*

MOORISH PROVERB

STEPPING OFF

A DAMP WIND BLEW up from the Mediterranean Sea, cooling me a little as I stood on the small balcony and watched turbaned men, donkeys, and mini-pickup trucks weaving through the evening crowds in the north Algerian port of Oran. It was getting dark and the songs of various muezzin called the people to prayer, long and high-pitched, echoing out over the city. Around the central square, small neon signs flashed tightly wound Arabic letters. Orange coals glowed in the food stand grills, smoke carrying the smell of cooking meat into the air.

It was my very first night in Algeria after a few harried days in Morocco trying to figure out some way to get across the desert into sub-Saharan Africa. On the advice of some tired-looking British tourists at the Moroccan border I had taken an all-day bus to Oran, and then bought another ticket for a bus leaving early in the morning to go south to Ghardaia on the northern edge of the vast Sahara. I was trying to enjoy the excitement of the moment, but as I stood by myself, surrounded by strange sights and smells and sounds, a thousand thoughts were whirling through my head. I couldn't quite see the Mediterranean waters out beyond the buildings and beyond the cliffs leading down to the port, but the space was there — a great, black void below the stars that I knew would be my last familiar reference point for a long while. In the morning I would turn my back on the sea and on Europe, where I had been backpacking for two months, and step off into places and experiences completely new and unknown.

Inside the room, as I washed the day's sweat and dust off my face and neck, I regretted that I had been unable to find any books to read about traveling in the Sahara. Too many things in north Africa felt strange and unfamiliar.

I wish there were a few other tourists around to go to dinner with, I thought, or a few more people outside who looked like me. I dug into my pack for my lightweight red, white, and blue running jacket, took a deep breath, and went out to get some food and see a bit of the city.

In the streets, everything was a mixture of old and new, Arab and Western. Half of the people were in pants and dresses, while the other half were wearing traditional Muslim cloaks and turbans. Some of the buildings had arches and decorative Moorish scrolling, others showed their French colonial roots, and still others were an uninspired combination of cinder block and corrugated tin roofing. There were donkey-drawn carts and women carrying large bundles under the billboards and neon signs.

Oran was a fairly modern, ordered city — especially after the chaos of Morocco — but there were strong undercurrents of tension. As I walked around, truckloads of soldiers occasionally sped through the streets, their helmets and rifles flashing under the streetlamps. Many of the locals hurried along stone-faced or huddled quietly in small groups. Near the public buildings downtown

I was surprised to find billboards depicting battle scenes from the war for independence fought thirty years earlier. One particularly graphic billboard showed fierce Algerians storming the walls of a French fort, skewering legionnaires with their bayonets. I was marveling at the gruesome details of this picture and others like it in the plâce 1 Novembre when two brawling men, surrounded by a pack of cheering onlookers, came careening down the empty sidewalk. A garbage truck turned down the street and the work-men hanging on the back were so pleased by the scene that they threw trash can lids into the crowd just to get in on the action. I quickly slipped off in the other direction.

I headed along the edge of the downtown area, looking out at the water and the boats tied up in the port, trying not to worry too much about the road ahead. But I couldn't help wondering about the confluence of impulses that had led me to this place. Just a few months before, I had been working steadily, moving along in a budding film career in Baltimore and Washington, D.C. At a sum-mer barbecue a friend had innocuously mentioned a letter from one of our fraternity brothers who was in the Peace Corps. "Come see me in Africa," the letter said. "We'll hang out in Timbuktu and hitchhike across the Sahara."

There had been some lighthearted joking about a few of us packing up and heading off, but as time went by I found myself more and more captivated by the idea. A few years before I had set off to go around the world with one of my college friends, but we had gotten only as far east as Palestine before we ran out of money, got homesick, and flew back in time for Christmas. Our monthlong stay on an Israeli kibbutz had included a trip to Egypt, and from the Giza plateau I had seen the Saharan dunes rolling into the distant space beyond the pyramids. My friend Ian and I had joked about commandeering a camel to plunge off into that ocean of sand. Without my realizing it, the notion had taken root and grown in me even before "hitchhiking in the Sahara" was ever mentioned at the barbecue.

For the rest of the summer and into the fall, while I worked fourteen- and sixteen-hour days doing support work on big movie sets, I kept daydreaming about those great open sand dunes, and about the animal-filled plains and wild jungles of Africa. What I hadn't seen or read about, I filled in with images from some of my favorite movies — Lawrence of Arabia, Born Free, Out of Africa. Ironically, the lyrical imagery and otherworldliness of these movies had been part of my inspiration to pursue a career in film. For a few years I had been trying to learn everything I could about making movies. But I was getting tired of wrestling industrial air-conditioning ducts close enough to the set to keep Tom Selleck comfortable, and worrying about the perils of clapping the sync marker too close to Jessica Lange's nose. I had learned a great deal and met some fascinating characters, but I needed some time to digest what I had learned and to remember why I had gotten into the business in the first place.

And besides, I was feeling generally tired of America — tired of the crowded highways and endless traffic lights, tired of the self-serving bickering in politics, tired of the unattended decay and poverty of downtown Baltimore and Washington. In college, I had been more reluctant than most to let go of my Catholic school ideals of how the world could work, and the postcollege world had made the dissonance between ideal and reality even more acute.

In late October (just five days after finishing my third exhausting film in a row), with little solid preparation and no concrete itinerary, I spent $139 on a one-way ticket from AirHitch and flew from New York to Paris. For a month and a half I toured Italy, France, and Spain, visiting churches, art galleries, small towns, and museums. Along the way, I tried to figure out how to get to sub-Saharan Africa without spending a fortune, and where to go once I got there. I pored over the State Department reports I had picked up before leaving and read the few African travel books I had been able to find (one about a guy hiking around a lake in Chad, another about a couple paying bribes and getting stuck in mud holes as they tried to drive through central Africa in a beat-up VW). As I traveled through France and Italy, I was so focused on Africa that people I met along the way would sometimes get annoyed that I was not taking my European travel more seriously. I even declined to go up the leaning tower in Pisa one afternoon (not knowing they would close it to tourists five months later), choosing instead to sit in the shade of the Duomo and read an article about corruption and ethnic strife in Nigeria. A college girl I had met at the hostel in Florence snapped at me, "Why don't you just head to Africa now. You'd obviously prefer to be over there."

But in addition to planning a route, I had to get visas and finish getting vaccinations for cholera, typhoid, yellow fever, and hepatitis. When I finally figured out that I would have to go through Algeria if I was going to cross the Sahara, a U.S. consular officer in Paris told me I would have to get an additional passport. "They won't let you in if they see your stamp for Israel," he told me. "They'll refuse your visa and never tell you why." So I had to wait another week in Paris for a special temporary passport and the Algerian visa, time I spent watching films at the Centre Pompideau, touring every museum I could find, and even stirring up a little romance at the hostel. By the time I made my way south into Spain and Portugal I could almost converse in French with some of the locals. At least I could order a *croque monsieur*, ask directions, and inquire about vacancies and room prices.

When I crossed the Strait of Gibraltar in mid-December, huge storm clouds were billowing on the horizon and the sea was gray and choppy. A cold wind blew spray into the air. When everyone went inside I made myself stay out on the deck, watching the coast of Spain receding slowly and the coast of North Africa growing by the minute. Why does this voyage seem so necessary to me, I wondered? Why does it seem so essential for me to test myself like this, alone out in the world? Why am I so drawn to the songs and rhythms and colors of such faraway cultures?

There had never been any effort to breed artists or adventur-
ers in my family, but occasionally they had sprung up. On my
mother's side, my eighty-nine-year-old Aunt Winifred, who grew
up in a small Kansas town that was pioneered by her grandmother,
had turned away many suitors after falling in love with travel at a
young age. Until she got too old, she had gone off every few years
to exotic places around the globe, returning with knickknacks,
stories, and a thousand memories that sustained her long after her
traveling days ended. She alone among my family had been gen-
uinely pleased when I announced my plans to go around the
world. On my father's side, my great-great-uncle Colonel Ben
Burbridge was among the early white hunters in Africa in the
1910s and 1920s. He became known for bringing the first live
mountain gorillas back from the Belgian Congo, both to Belgium
and to the U.S. My grandmother had occasionally told stories
about his fortitude and tenacity, how he spent weeks alone in the
jungle trying to meet pygmies and cannibals, and how he once
smuggled young gorillas onto French trains after landing at
Marseilles. He had even kept an adult gorilla for years at his
brother's home on the St. Johns River near Jacksonville, Florida,
attracting the country's top behavioral scientists, and more than
once alarming the neighbors.

Perhaps those stories had gotten under my skin. But as I stood
alone, looking out at the Mediterranean Sea in northern Algeria,
I found myself feeling a little low on both fortitude and tenacity. I
could only hope that I had inherited more than just the remote
impulses toward adventure.

I made my way back to the square near my hotel and bought
some grilled vegetables and couscous at a shish kebab stand.
Everything had quieted down. The evening crowds had gone
home for the night. I ate slowly and went back up to my room. It
felt stark and lonely — the floors a dirty green and white lin-
oleum, the mattress low and thin and covered with an old red and
black wool blanket. I checked the sheets and although they

weren't quite white, they seemed to have been recently washed. It wasn't a great place, but at least it was a hotel room, and I hadn't had many on the trip.

I repacked my backpack, trying to organize everything to be compact and accessible. My lightweight tent, sleeping bag, and stove were all in the bottom stuff-sack pocket. My waterproof, fleece-lined parka was tucked away under the rest of the wardrobe — a couple of T-shirts, a pair of jeans, a pair of shorts, a pair of khaki "convertibles" with zip-off legs that could be worn short or long, some thermal underwear, a couple of pairs of boxers, and a few pairs of socks. In a small day pack that zipped onto the larger pack I had my journal and other papers, a guide to sub-Saharan West Africa, and all of my valuables including both passports, a camera, compact binoculars, and a small stockpile of medicines. On the advice of a French doctor, I had already starting taking antimalarial pills every day, though it felt a little foolish since I was heading into the desert.

With the bag all packed I sat on the bed and tried to read, but my mind kept wandering. I could feel anxiety tugging at me again, bringing doubts about what I was doing. Go back to the Costa del Sol and spend a little time on the beach, a voice was saying. Go back to Paris and see some more films; go to Rouvenac and help Laurent finish his sheep barn. You could go to Egypt and take a ship straight to Kenya or go back to Lisbon and take a boat to the Canary Islands, and then to Senegal. All the options that I had dismissed now seemed much more feasible than crossing into the Sahara. What happens if you get halfway and can't get any more rides, I wondered? What happens if you get in with some unseemly characters and you have no way of escape, let alone protecting yourself?

But somewhere deep inside I was pretty sure that I was headed in the right direction. The quiet voice that had urged me to set out in the first place and led me across the Strait of Gibraltar had practically yelled, "Yes!" every time I looked at a map of the

Sahara. I wasn't sure that I could make it all the way across, but I had followed my instincts this far and I was at least going to give it a good shot.

At four in the morning, I dragged myself out of bed, pulled on my pack, and set out for the bus station. I didn't get very far before I was wide awake. When I had made plans the day before to catch the 5:00 AM bus, I had expected that dawn would be breaking and I would have a peaceful walk through early morning Oran. Instead it was still night and there were shadows and whispering voices everywhere. The shops were closed with steel gates in front; people huddled in many of the doorways and alleys. It was so dark in some places that I almost tripped over bodies I hadn't seen sleeping on the sidewalk.

Any last vestige of confidence from the night before vanished. I was seized with a dark, overriding sense of fear. Soon I was lost and had to ask directions from a woman scurrying by, and then from a young man who came rattling down the street on an old bike. I crisscrossed the streets, moving from one side to the other whenever I saw a group of men who looked dangerous. Three times I nearly turned back, standing paralyzed on the sidewalk, unable to decide whether to go forward or not. But each time I went on.

Finally, after forty minutes, I happened upon the station. It was brightly lit and crowded with people waiting for the bus, among them two couples who were backpackers like myself. I sat on my pack in a corner, feeling wrung out and a little foolish for getting so worked up. The couples were laughing and casually joking around, while I sat there pale and rattled. I couldn't talk to anyone.

You are some intrepid traveler, I thought to myself, the last of the true stalwarts. Most of the Algerians looked dark and inhospitable to me, their eyes deeply set, their wrinkled faces hard to read. It was all too different, too foreign. My stomach sank. I felt like I was banishing myself to a desolate outpost rather than setting out on a great adventure, but I knew I couldn't turn back. I had thought about and dreamed about traveling through the desert and through Africa too many times to let the notion go. And so anxiety gave way to fatalism, and when the bus came, I stowed my bag in the hold and got on, stepping into the unknown with a blindness that I had never experienced before.

SOLITUDE

THE SUN ROSE AS THE BUS CLIMBED onto the high plateau south of Oran, heading into the Algerian extension of the Atlas mountains. Expecting only desert, I was soon surprised to find a lush plain containing wheat, corn, and herds of goats and sheep. In a few of the villages Muslim prayers rang out from the small minarets, announcing the morning. A short while later, the villages we passed through began coming to life with schoolchildren and donkey-drawn carts ambling down the sunny streets. My anxieties lightened as we went along, a sense of relief and surety building throughout the day. I found myself increasingly happy to be moving south, away from the crowded coast. The bus cruised along for hours, stopping in the little farming towns, and I kept thinking, I am going. Now I am really going. I felt like an adventurer, researcher, and time traveler, all rolled into one. I felt like a diver bouncing high at the edge of a board, ready to fly into some wondrous dive. Having moved beyond my foreseeable plans, I began to feel the thrill of truly exploring.

In the afternoon we passed over the Saharan Atlas range near Laghouat. The windswept grass became progressively drier; the landscape turned brown and barren. The air grew hotter and in its dryness I could almost taste the desert coming. The towns dwindled and the farms disappeared, leaving only sheep and goats ranging over the dusty hills, nibbling on scrubby bushes. I kept expecting to see rolling dunes, but instead there were rocky hills and plateaus cutting off the horizons.

Late in the afternoon, the bus started a long, winding descent through steep canyons into the ancient oasis town of Ghardaia. I could see palm trees toward the center of town, but much of the city had spilled into the desert beyond the old water source. "After Ghardaia, begin Sahara," a raisinlike old man at the bus station told me when I tried to ask about getting rides further south. "Now Sahara, Sahara," he kept saying, pointing south. I wasn't sure if he didn't understand me or if he was trying to tell me that I shouldn't expect to get much further.

I noticed that the other tourists were heading off together, so I put on my pack and followed them up the road. There was a campground for Westerners a mile and a half north of the bus station, well apart from the rest of the town. As the sun set, I put my tent up in an empty corner away from the handful of other campers. I lit my small stove and cooked some soup mixed with tomatoes, onions, and rice, and then ate it slowly, feeling the temperature drop as the light faded. I was studying my Michelin map by candlelight, contemplating the unpopulated stretches below Ghardaia, when I began to catch parts of a melody floating over from a nearby camp. It was German, but the tune was unmistakable. The words came into my mind slowly: "Silent night . . . Holy night . . ." I hadn't even realized that it was Christmas Eve.

I looked up at the stars layered across the sky, positioned as at home but far more numerous. I thought of my family all together with a roaring fire and stockings hanging above the fireplace; the twinkling lights on the tree and the presents underneath, a football game on the television. I thought of the piles of turkey, stuffing, mashed potatoes, and gravy. Surrounded by sand and strangers, I felt a loneliness more intense than any I had ever known. Tears dropped onto my map and I could not keep my body from shaking. Unable to suppress the feelings, I finally went inside my tent and lay down with my thoughts. I had vivid dreams of home that night, with family and friends from elementary school, high school, and college. I ran around all night with almost everyone I had ever known in a kind of half party, half battle against some indiscernible foe. It was the first of many such hyperkinetic dreams that the sparse desert would bring.

On Christmas Day I wrote letters home, mailed them at a post office in town, and stocked up on provisions — canned soup, sardines, bottled water, some vegetables, and bananas. I was not sure if there would be much food beyond Ghardaia. The next day, I got up early, walked a short ways down the road with my hand out, and quickly caught a ride with a French petroleum engineer and his Algerian assistant. They were driving a little Russian Neva and were on their way to check some oil wells near Ouargla in the east. We flew along the rocky, hard-packed desert, usually a few hundred yards from the rutted main track, testing the car and the driver's abilities as he tried to push it over seventy-five miles an hour. I was hunched in the small backseat, the warm wind blasting me as we went.

The engineer spoke English and he kept turning around in his seat while he drove to tell me stories of his experiences in the oil fields of Algeria and Libya. He was going to spend three weeks driving from oil rig to oil rig and then he would go back to his farmhouse outside of Marseilles. He seemed ecstatic to be back in the desert again. If he could just figure out a way to slip over the border into Libya to see the Paris-Dakar Rally, he said, the trip would be perfect. After a couple of hours, they announced that it was

time for them to turn east. There were no tracks in that direction
or any clear markings that I saw, but they were not concerned.

"No problem. We have water. We have gasoline and we have
a compass," the engineer said while his friend smiled.

They waited with me until we were able to flag down a small
white pickup heading my way. The driver was a young Algerian
mechanic named Yousef and he seemed perfectly pleased to have
me hop in. He was on his way home from Oran with used engine
parts he had just purchased for his garage. As we pulled out, I
watched the Neva bouncing off into the desert to the east. It
looked as if the two oil men were headed toward the edge of the
earth. At least to the south we had the comfort of an intermittently paved road. It was usually closed "for military use only,"
but driving on the nearby hard-packed piste was often just as
smooth.

For the rest of the day, Yousef and I drove along talking in a
mixture of French and English. The terrain was mostly rock and
dirt: perfectly flat for twenty or thirty miles, then canyons and
mesas and worn hills, followed by more flat dirt and gravel. There
were no towns and no side roads, only widely spaced gas stations
with sparse restaurants selling local soda pop and meager food that
got more expensive the further south we went.

After noon, we stopped at one of these restaurants and Yousef
insisted on buying me lunch. When I told him sincerely that I
would prefer to buy him lunch since he was giving me a ride, he
laughed heartily.

"This is Algeria. You are my guest," he said. He didn't seem
very well-off and I did not want to accept, but he was so cheerfully
insistent that I felt I had to. We ate pita bread and seasoned rice
and talked about the desert as best we could. We had passed several herds of semiwild camels and he told me that they wander
about the desert at will and meet up with their nomadic owners
every three or four years. The Tuareg nomads, he said, often live
in the desert on two dates and just three or four swallows of water

a day, and they can recognize their own camels from two kilometers away. He told me about his life as a mechanic, fixing cars for
tourists and oil teams in the small town of Adrar on the other
north-south route from Morocco to Mali. He was very proud of his
town and wanted me to come see it, but he said that for hitchhiking, the route that I was on was much better. To my great relief, he said he thought I would have no trouble getting across.

"If you are standing alone in the desert, who will pass you by?"
he asked with a reassuring smile.

In midafternoon we stopped near the top of a ridge because it
was past time for midday prayers. I climbed a small hill to get a
view of the surroundings. Nearby a herd of goats foraged about.
Down below I could see Yousef going through the Muslim ritual of
washing his hands and face, bending his forehead to the ground
between careful splashes of water from his canteen. He settled
into his prayer, facing east-southeast across the barren land toward
Mecca. Between us and the holy city there is almost nothing but
rock and sand, I thought: a couple thousand miles of desert, then
the Nile, more desert, the Red Sea, and then Mecca. Yousef
looked tiny, yet perfectly at home in the vast surroundings and I
had an impulse to kneel on the rocky ground and join him in his
ancient ritual. Instead I turned slowly in circles, soaking in the
view from every direction, unable to resist a few silent prayers of
my own.

Late in the afternoon we saw some of the first Saharan dunes
in vast ranges, first on one side of the road, then on the other.
They were high and wide with a rich orange-yellow coloring.
They moved constantly, Yousef told me, about five miles a year,
sometimes covering a paved section of the road and then reveal-
ing it again two years later. He was very happy to see them again
because it meant that he was nearing home. God willing, he said,
he would be home that night before his wife went to sleep.

We passed through the oasis town of El Golea, a sudden patch
of green in the brown desert, with thousands of tall palm trees. It

was the last town on the map for 250 miles, but we didn't even stop. My driver was on a mission, and I was happy to be on the mission with him. I wanted to keep going as far as I could.

A few hours later we came to a crossroads where Yousef had to turn west. There were only two east-west roads that connected the north-south routes, and this was one of them. There was a gas station operated by three tattered-looking men. A few miles to the north there was a line of big dunes. In every other direction, there was nothing.

As the pickup truck pulled away the three men stared at me, dumbfounded. I bought an orange soda and then waited forty-five minutes by the road, continually distracted by the dunes as I watched for another vehicle coming from the north. No one came. I bought another soda and drank it while they watched me. Then I put my pack on my shoulders, gave them a wave, and started hiking off toward the dunes. The sun was starting to set and I was tired enough now that I didn't even want another ride. The dunes looked too great to pass up. Walking towards their high, golden hills I felt like I was in a dream. The sound of my shoes scuffing against the rocks seemed distant in the vast open space.

The dunes were considerably larger and farther away than I had thought. When I finally climbed up into them forty minutes later, I experienced a sense of visceral, tactile delight that I hadn't felt in a long time. The sand was warm and so fine that it was almost silky. I hiked over a couple of ridges so that I would be well out of sight, sliding down each time between them, nearly falling as I followed the little avalanches I was causing. I put my tent up in a small valley between the dunes. It was still light on one side, with a growing shadow on the other. For a moment I sat and listened. There was nothing — only my breathing. I could almost hear my heart pounding.

I explored a bit, checking out the views from the highest dunes. To the east the ground was rocky and flat. To the west there was a sea of sand, the yellow dunes rolling to the horizon. Everything was so smooth and fluid that I felt almost guilty disturbing it, but I couldn't resist the urge to dive and slide down a few of the slopes. I stepped out my initials in huge letters on the face of one and leveled the ridge line of another with avalanching steps, watching the sand cascade all the way to the bottom. I started to feel a little foolish and self-conscious, but all I had to do was look around to realize that there was no one to see me.

As I watched the sun sink in the west, elegant divisions of dark and light were sculpted along the snaking ridges all around. In the dunes near my tent, I made a point of retracing my footsteps, taking care not to spoil the smoothness of the surrounding walls. The light dropped quickly and a slight breeze blew cooler by the minute. Sitting between the dunes, with no sound other than the breeze, the silence was overwhelming. It was like listening to the inside of a shell, perhaps like being in a shell, looking out with no view but the sky.

As it got dark, I thought about snakes and other desert critters waking for the night, so I crawled into the safety of my tent and cooked some rice and vegetables in my open vestibule. Outside, a blanket of stars swept above my head. Some blended together into clouds of light, while others loomed so large and so bright that they seemed within reach. I felt I might be able to grab a handful to hold in my pocket, and at the same time, I felt as tiny as the grains of sand around me. I was far away now from the crowded cities. With the cover of my tent off so that I could see the sky through the screened roof, I lay down to think, nestled in my warm sleeping bag and enveloped in an infinite cradle of sand and stars.

It had taken me a while to realize that part of the reason for the trip had been a desire to be alone, to have some time to think for a bit, to reorganize things and reorient my inner compass. Traveling, I was finding, was really stripping me down and opening me up in ways that I hadn't expected, especially when I was alone. Outside of my culture, away from my friends and my routines, constantly experiencing new smells and sights and ideas, I had become naked and impressionable. But the questions of home were always there, bouncing off the things I was seeing and hearing, reordering themselves as I went. Where did I want to go with my career? What was I really passionate about? How could I find a sense of contentment and fulfillment in work, in the place I lived, in relationships, in myself? I had wanted to immerse myself in the aesthetics of other places, but the more I did so, the more I found myself looking back toward home and looking inward at myself. In traveling, I was finding, the desire for new experiences was always balanced by the longing for home; the quest for external experience always joined by inner revelation.

I had wanted to just go out and have fun learning and walking through the world, but instead I found myself fighting fear and loneliness, and seesawing between euphoria and despondency. In my small tent I could feel the isolation of the darkness, and I couldn't help but wonder if there were any nomads sneaking up nearby, or poisonous critters burrowing near the door. But somehow, out in the desert, those fears didn't seem as daunting as those I had experienced just a few days before. Alone in the dunes, I already felt stronger inside and clearer about the road I was taking.

CLOSE CALL

I WOKE UP AT FIRST LIGHT, thankful that nothing had emerged from the sand to bite me in the night. I ate some bread and packed up, still hungry but enjoying being surrounded by the smooth yellow sand. It was like waking up on another planet, a lone survivor stranded in another world. I hated to climb back out of my sand valley, but even on the other side of the dune a fascinating world awaited. Before the sun rose — it begins getting light in the Sahara long before the sun comes up — I started walking toward the road.

As I climbed down the last dune to the rocky ground that stretched to the east, I could just see a trail of dust rising far off to the north. It looked like it could be a truck heading south. I picked up my pace, hoping to at least get near the main track before the vehicle passed. To the south I could see a single light on at the little gas station–café. I had figured I would just walk there again to wait for a ride, but I ended up reaching the road about thirty seconds before the truck came rolling by. It was an oil truck driven by a paunchy, jovial Algerian. He stopped for me more out of surprise and concern than anything else, but he was perfectly happy to give me a ride. We stopped at the little station for some breakfast and the men there seemed amused that he had picked me up. They spoke to each other in Arabic and looked at me and laughed.

"You are knowing my friend Yousef Beni?" the driver said to me when we got back in the truck. "Yousef Beni is bringing you here last night."

"Yes," I said. "You know Yousef?"

"Yes, yes. This man is my good friend, the best mechanic in the Sahara," the driver said, "It is good for you. Yousef Beni is a very good man."

The paved road that had started just a mile before the station ended just a mile beyond it, and the going became much slower than it had been the previous days. For fourteen hours we bounced along on rocky track, listening to cacophonous Arabic music, taking all day to go less than two-hundred-and-fifty miles. My driver kept asking if I liked the different songs. Most of them were pretty awful and he would get a big kick out of it when I told him that a particular song was no good. "It is very bad," I would say, grimacing at the the noise as he roared with delight, more so if it were a Moroccan or Tunisian song. But he would also beam when I found some that I liked, especially if they were Algerian songs.

"Algerian music is best in the world," he told me proudly.

He left me off just north of In Salah, another oasis town deep in the desert, and then he turned west to go deliver his load. It was dark when he let me off and I was exhausted, so I just pitched my tent near the road. I could hear a few dogs barking and the occasional murmur of voices, but no one seemed to be nearby. I went straight to sleep and got up early the next morning, worried that I might be on someone's property. Sure enough, about three hundred yards away was an adobe-style shack with a small stream of blue smoke coming from the chimney and lumps of rubbish scattered around the yard. But land is not a big issue in the Sahara. Even in the occasional towns, real estate is not something in short supply. If I had been drinking from someone's well, I might have had cause to worry.

In the faint light I could see other buildings of the town rising up on a bluff to the west and the road curving southeast. The asphalt had begun again about two miles before the town, and from the dark line on my map it looked like it would go for about fifty miles to the south. Remembering the rugged track from the day before, I hoped it would. But I had already learned that the paved sections were like mercurial friends coming and going on a whim — and often worse than the numerous well-worn tracks nearby.

I packed up and walked sleepily along the road toward the south. For a long while the town of In Salah didn't seem to get closer, just bigger. What I had thought were single houses on the ridges above the town grew into lines of colorful adobes, all clustered together. In big American cities, houses piled so close always seem to be squeezing each other, pushing and shoving for room. But here, with the endless space all around, the houses gave the impression of huddling together for comfort and survival. As I walked along the edge of the town none of the shops were open and only a few groggy souls were stirring. I had wanted to buy some more food and water, but I decided not to wait for things to open, figuring there would still be plenty of gas station–cafés along the way. I wanted to find a good hitching spot just south of town and get set up before anyone went by. I had been lucky with rides so far, but the traffic was getting so sparse — maybe ten or fifteen vehicles passing a day — that I didn't want to risk missing any possibilities.

When I finally got to the southern edge of town, where all of the roads came together into the one highway, I set my pack down and stretched my shoulders, feeling good and awake, warm inside against the cold air. Then I noticed something stirring next to the road, fifty yards away. It was a large dark, hairy object that was moving slowly, almost like a bear. My pulse tripled instantly. I couldn't imagine what it was. But then it sat up blinking — one of the darkest men I had ever seen. He stood up, at least six-and-a-half-feet tall. His kinky hair was dusty and unruly, sticking out in clumps and without even dusting himself off he pulled the long brown cloak that he had been using as a blanket over his head. He smiled and started walking toward me. I greeted him using one of the few Arabic words I had learned: "Asalamo."

"Asalamo alaïkoum," he said. His large eyes surveyed the surroundings, blinking in the early light. He yawned broadly and spoke again in Arabic.

"I'm sorry, I don't speak Arabic," I said in English. "Vous parlez francais?"

He hesitated. "Oui."

"Ah, bon," I said, "Je parle un peu de francais." He smiled and nodded, but I could tell that he hadn't fully understood.

"Dormez-vous ici?" I asked. He blinked at me a moment and then caught the meaning.

"Oui," he said, motioning towards the desert, he had slept out there.

"Il fait froid?" I asked, thinking that it must have been horribly cold without a tent or sleeping bag. He just shrugged as if to say, "no problem." The wind blew and a shiver ran through me as the sweat began to cool on my back. He pulled the big hood of his cloak over his head, but didn't seem cold at all. His cloak looked like it was made of dark brown horse or camel hair. He looked like a monk with the hood on, the sleeves covering his hands and the bottom just dragging on the ground so that it was worn and tattered around the edges. His feet were bare and flattened and cracked like the end of a chewed twig. He had a worn leather purse with him and nothing else.

"Voyagez-vous seule?" he asked.

"Oui," I said, I was traveling alone. He raised his eyebrows, surprised.

"And you?" I asked.

"Oui," he said, nodding his head, looking up and down the road, as if he wasn't entirely sure which direction he was headed.

"Où allez vous?" he asked. I didn't quite understand him. He pointed down the road stretching endlessly to the south, "Où?"

I realized he was asking where I was headed. "Mali." I told him.

"Mali? Mali c'est l'autre route," he said, pointing toward the west. "Cette route va a Niger."

I tried to explain that first I was going to Niger, then Mali, adding that I had a friend who lived in Mali.

"Votre ami?" he said. "Ah, bon."

"Et vous?" I asked, wondering where he was headed.

Again he looked up and down the road, looking kind of sad. "Abelessa — tout près Tamanrasset — pour visite à ma famille." I hoped that he was telling the truth, that he had family in the south, but something told me he didn't. He didn't look like any of the Algerians I had seen. I was curious about him, but my French wasn't good enough to find out much. As the call to prayers started faintly, then loudly in town, I asked him if we should try to get a ride together. He declined, saying that it would be bad for me. He walked on up the road a few hundred yards and stood with his eyes closed facing straight east. I couldn't tell if he was warming his face or praying or even sleeping again standing up. A pair of four-wheel-drive jeeps came by carrying tourists, loaded with spare tires and extra gas tanks. They seemed embarrassed to pass me, averting their eyes or shrugging their shoulders apologetically. By the time they got to him, they were gunning their engines up to full speed.

I could hear any motor coming from way off and I would watch eagerly for the car or truck to appear. I could hear the town begin to come alive and see people and animals moving around in the streets. A couple of tanker trucks came by and then a green military transport truck, with big sand tires, stopped to offer me a ride. The young soldier driving smiled and waved me in as I opened the door. He was in his midthirties, about ten years older than me. I greeted him in Arabic and then asked in French if there was room for my friend, pointing down the road to where he stood like a statue.

"No, no," the driver said hurriedly, patting the seat and revving his engine to keep it from stalling.

He said something in Arabic that I interpreted as, "If you are coming, get in because I don't have all day." I heaved my pack up onto the floor of the cab and climbed in. As we pulled off, I waved to the man in the cloak. I saw him watching us with his eyes as we passed, but he did not move his head and he did not wave. I hoped that I would run into him further down the road, but I never saw him again.

As we drove along, the Algerian soldier began talking up a storm. He seemed far too awake considering the hour. At first he spoke in Arabic, but then he switched to French. Still I could only understand a quarter of what he said. I asked what he was carrying and where he was going, but I couldn't decipher much from his answers. He kept motioning toward the vast desert to the west and seemed to be saying that he was eventually going somewhere remote in that direction. But he made it clear that he would first be going south for a while. I smiled and nodded, trying to participate in his monologue. I felt a wave of sleepiness come over me as the sun heated the dashboard and the large tires hummed on the asphalt.

He finally grew quiet, and for a while I dozed until the truck went off the pavement. We bounced along the track parallel to the asphalt as I had done with many of my rides, usually because the pavement was reserved for military vehicles. I tried to make a joke by asking him if the paved road was reserved for tourists. "No, this is better," he said in French. His voice sounded a little strange and I noticed that his breathing had become shorter and quicker. He glanced at me twice and looked away when he saw me looking at him. I looked straight ahead as my mind raced, watching him out of the corner of my eye. He shifted uncomfortably in his seat, adjusting his pants.

Oh, shit, I thought. Shit! How could I have been so stupid as to have gotten into a truck with some lonely soldier? I could hear his breathing getting louder, he was almost gasping. Twice before I had seen men acting like this — an old man in a library when I was in high school, who had taken a friendly interest in my work and then misunderstood my own friendliness, and a professor who had offered to give me a personal tour of the gym on my very first day at college. Both times I had been extremely naive, not really understanding what their intentions had been until thinking things through afterward. But this time I knew instantly. For months, my biggest fear about the trip had been the possibility of being abducted and raped by a bunch of nomads in the middle of the Sahara. Maybe because I had seen *Lawrence of Arabia,* or because of something I had read, or just because of some internal long-range warning system, it was something I had worried about a number of times.

But I hadn't worried enough. Clearly. The soldier started to move uncomfortably in his seat and he had to swerve to miss a small bush. I looked over and saw that he had just unbuckled his pants and that he was pulling down the zipper. He glanced at me with a desperate, blind look on his face and then back at the road, seeming to go faster as he pulled at his pants, trying to get them down.

"Qu'est-ce que c'est?" I asked angrily, trying to say, what are you doing?, "Qu'est-ce que c'est!"

He looked at me like a child, shocked and startled, as if I had snuck up on him, "Quoi?" he asked lamely.

"What the hell do you think you're doing?" I said in English, losing my French for a second, "C'est mauvais! C'est mauvais pour

moi." I was trying to convey that I was angry and definitely not interested. But I didn't want to escalate the situation. I wanted to
defuse it.

He seemed to get it. He mumbled something and pulled his
pants back up, trying to refocus on the road as he buttoned them.
He seemed hurt and embarrassed and truly sorry, but I was still
worried. I glanced carefully around the cab to see if there was a gun
or any other weapon anywhere. I didn't see any and he wasn't
wearing any kind of holster, even for a knife, though I was figuring
he must have weapon if he was a soldier.

"Arret, s'il vous plait," I said, asking him to stop the truck,
"Arret, ici."

He started to slow down, but instead of stopping he began
apologizing profusely.

"C'est d'accord," I told him, "C'est pas pour moi, c'est tout."
It just wasn't something for me.

He nodded his head vigorously saying that he understood.
There was a café just ten minutes ahead, he said and he started ac-
celerating again. It was a much better place for getting a ride and
I could get breakfast too. He would help me get a ride.

"Ten minutes?" I asked.

"Oui, dix minutes. No problem," he said. I sat back and stared
out the window, stewing, thinking it was done. But after fifteen
minutes when I asked him where the café was he responded angrily. He had been stewing too. He said it was just ahead, but then
he started saying things in Arabic, sounding threatening and motioning off into the desert on either side.

My stomach lurched. I knew that he could drive twenty miles
off the road in either direction and if he had any way to over-
power me, I would probably never even be found. From his tone
and his gestures, I worried that he might be considering exactly
that. I decided to get my Swiss army knife out. I picked up my
small shoulder pack and placed it on my lap with the pockets
away from him.

"Where is the café?" I asked him.

He didn't say anything. I noticed his breathing had become shallow again. Oh, shit. Here we go, I thought, knowing that this time there would be no pretense of misunderstanding, no easy outs. I asked again where the café was.

"Near," he said breathlessly, nodding up ahead, wide-eyed, "It's very near."

He was grabbing himself now, squeezing the outside of his pants. I slowly unzipped the front pocket of my pack and flipped the knife over in the pocket, feeling for the leather punch at the top edge. It was pointy like a toothpick, but as thick as a screwdriver. With my left hand I pulled the spike upright, perpendicular to the rest of the knife. Then I took the knife out, concealing it in my fist. I could hear him breathing heavily and when I looked at him he was looking around at the desert on either side, wild-eyed. In one motion he unbuttoned and unzipped his pants again and began sliding them down. I shifted the knife to my right hand and gripped it firmly with the spike sticking out between the two middle fingers of my fist. I had been kidding with friends before I left that if I ever needed one, this leather punch could turn into a dangerous weapon. I hadn't really thought I would ever need to use it.

He looked over at me when I shifted the knife. He looked alarmed and craned his head to see what I was holding. I could feel my adrenaline rising. I knew that if he made a move to turn off the main track or to pull a weapon from somewhere, that I would have to move fast and hope that someone would come along to help. If I let him get us out off the main track, I would be entirely on my own.

He had a pathetic look on his face as he looked to see what was in my hand. Though I had been able to stay pretty calm and think clearly, strong anger now welled up inside me.

"You want to know what this is?" I said in English, glaring at him. "It's a fucking knife, that's what. It's a knife. And I'm going to pop you right in the throat with it if you make one move." I didn't show it to him. I was angry, but I didn't want to threaten him outright.

He said something in Arabic, pulling back, his voice high-pitched. Again he tried to pull his pants back up, but now he was too worried about what I was going to do.

"Stop here," I said coldly. "Stop the truck now."

"Non, non, non," he said, frightened, "Pas d'problème. Pas d'problème."

Suddenly on the left side of the road I saw five cars parked on a rise about a quarter of a mile away. Obviously there were Europeans camping out.

"Stop here!" I said emphatically, beginning to lean forward, seriously considering a move before we got by them.

"D'accord. D'accord," he said, holding up a hand and slowing the truck. I opened the door and grabbed my bag before he even stopped. He braked quickly, knowing I was ready to jump out. He started apologizing and tried to help me get my bag out, but I pulled it away quickly, unsure why he was grabbing it. He honked his horn and yelled something toward the campers, trying to show that he was being cooperative, that he hadn't meant to do anything wrong.

"C'est mauvais," I said pointing at him before I shut the door. He waved at me to go in front of the truck, but I waved him on. Finally I walked behind the truck because he wouldn't leave. As I walked up the hill, again he honked and yelled, like he was concerned for my safety and wasn't going to leave until I had another ride.

I could see the other tourists by their cars looking at me and talking. The earth between us was dark gravel, steadily sloping. The adrenaline dissipated and I felt very tired and foolish walking up the hill. I waved sluggishly and called out, "Bonjour." No one said anything. They turned back to their packing. As I got closer I wondered if they were going to close up their cars and take off before I got there. When I finally got up to the camp, they seemed hesitant to look at me. A moonfaced guy who was working under the hood of a white Peugeot wagon eventually put down his tools and came toward me smiling. "Bonjour," he said, offering his greasy hand, "Ça va?"

"Bonjour," I said. "C'est pas bien . . ." I tried to tell him in French that I had just had a "little problem" with the soldier, but that I was okay. From another Peugeot wagon nearby, a wiry, unshaven man came over and in a strange language that I thought was Danish or Norwegian the first man told him what I had said. They both laughed. I couldn't understand them except to hear, "anglais ou americain."

"I suppose you want a ride," the scruffy man said in English. "We have no room."

"I had some difficulty," I said, "If I can just go someplace where I can wait for a good ride, I would appreciate it."

A third man, tall, with a pleasant smile, came over and nodded at me. They conversed briefly in what I soon found out was actually Flemish. "Okay, you ride with him," the scruffy man finally said, pointing to the moonfaced mechanic, "But we can only take you as far as the Sands of Death, two or three hours from here. There you can get a ride. No one will pass you waiting there."

"Thank you," I said, smiling gratefully. The smell of their breakfast still hung in the air and I realized that I was very hungry. Next to one of the two little Renault V's, two women in their early twenties were trying to eat and pack up at the same time. The scruffy man, whom everyone called Henri, yelled at them in French and they replied with some sort of joke that made everyone laugh except him. A little apart from the others, a well-dressed couple seemed to be arguing as they packed up their Peugeot sedan.

Each of the cars was full of equipment and supplies, but both of the station wagons had room in front. When it was time to leave, I got into the white Peugeot feeling relieved, figuring that they wouldn't leave me at any place called "the Sands of Death." Depending on how far they were going, I hoped that getting a ride with them might partially redeem a pretty awful start to the day.

GOLDEN RULE OF THE DESERT

IN A MIXTURE OF FRENCH and English, I poured on all the charm I could muster as we drove along, knowing that if I could make a positive impression and seem like pretty good company, my easy-going driver would vouch for me when the time came. His name was Cristophe and he was a shy man who was a mechanic back in Belgium with his own garage where he serviced mostly Renaults and Peugeots — "the best cars in the world," he said. During my two-hour audition, I figured that the trick was to be friendly, but not pesky, and to sit quietly without seeming morose. From experience, I knew that there was nothing worse than an overly chatty or overly serious hitchhiker. We were the rear car in the caravan and it was fun barreling along behind everyone else, talking just occasionally. Though he was reluctant to talk about himself, Cristophe seemed to enjoy telling me about the others, and

having some company to help pass the time in the desolate surroundings.

He told me that their leader, the disheveled and ornery Henri,
was a regular customer of his who made yearly trips across the
desert to sell cars in Africa. The tall man in the little green
Renault V was his brother-in-law Ludo, a wealthy guy who had
decided to come on the trip for fun and adventure. The couple in
the sedan were Italians their group had found stranded two days
before. They were on a holiday fling through the desert, but they
were grossly unprepared. The man, he told me, didn't even know
how to clean his filters or intake valves. It had taken Cristophe
two hours to get them running again, and longer than that to get
the woman calmed down. She had been sure they were going to
die out in the hard-packed desert.

"They are lucky you found them," I said.

He smiled, obviously proud of himself. The danger of the
desert added a whole new dimension to his work. "It was very easy,
nothing really," he said.

"And how about the girls?" I asked, "Are they relatives?"

"Non," he said, "They are French, on vacation." He explained
that a friend of Henri's had pulled out at the last minute, saying
he couldn't afford the time. They had found the girls in Algiers
and talked them into driving the car to Tamanrasset where they
would either sell it or find another driver to take the car to
Niamey. That was all I needed to hear. I wanted to whoop and
holler and hug Cristophe, but instead I just smiled and watched
the open desert roll by.

When we got to the Sands of Death, Henri was immediately
out of his car, surveying the conditions, looking for the best route
through. It was the first deep sand to be negotiated by the cars, but
it was only two hundred yards across to rocky ground again.

"It used to be much worse," Henri said, sounding disappointed, "but you cannot be too careful. The sand can be deceiv-
ing." While he was arguing with the girls over whether or not he

should drive their car through the sand, four motorcycles and a couple of cars heading north came along and sped right through. A couple of the motorcycles almost spilled, more because they were distracted by all of us walking around than from the conditions. All of the vehicles looked ragged and worn, and from a quick glimpse, the people didn't look a whole lot better, their clothes dusty, dirty kiffiyahs around their heads.

"Germans," Henri said with disdain, angry that they hadn't even stopped to give him a report on conditions ahead. A truck rolled by heading south and then the two jeeps with tourists that I had seen earlier. One got stuck, but we quickly pushed them out. Henri studied their routes and then gave instructions to the drivers. Everyone was excited except for the Italian woman who stayed in her car, pouting. Her husband was wide-eyed and kept following Henri, asking him questions. As everyone returned to their cars I hoped that they would forget about leaving me off there.

But Henri pointed at me and said, "So, okay, this is the place for you. Do you have your bags?"

I wasn't sure how serious he was, but before I could answer, my driver Cristophe and his brother-in-law Ludo said something to Henri and they all had a quick conference to determine my fate. The discussion was animated, but I clearly had two allies. The tall man, Ludo, laughed and chomped on his cigar, giving me reassuring nods while Henri stormed back and forth, working his hand over his whiskers. Moonfaced Cristophe, who still had engine grease on his face from the morning, looked like a schoolkid trying to hold back laughter.

"We are getting too many people," Henri yelled in English to the general surroundings when they were finished. But then he came over to me and said, "Okay. He says you are a good man. You ride with us to the camping tonight. After that, we will see."

Cristophe patted me on the back and Ludo shook my hand, smiling around the cigar. Everyone made it through the sand without getting stuck except for the Italian couple, but we got them out easily and were soon on our way. We cruised along the rocky desert as fast as we could, dodging ruts and zipping through occasional patches of sand. We followed each other in a wide line, staggered sideways, so that each car would not get in the dust being kicked up by the ones in front. But still the dust came pouring in, giving me a headache and getting so deep into my hair that after a few hours it was sticking up all over. Cristophe and I were bringing up the rear so that Cristophe could help anyone who had car trouble. All day the sun got higher and hotter, leaving me parched and starting to feel dizzy. When I had stocked up on bottled water a few days before, I was surprised to find so many little places selling soda and food. Now that I had little food or water with me, I was surprised to find that through the whole day we hadn't see one place. There was nothing but desert now. No roads, no signs. In many places there wasn't even a discernible track, just occasional piles of rocks to mark the way.

In the middle of the afternoon, we stopped to help dig out an oil truck that was stuck in soft sand. For two hours we went through the tedious process of digging the sand from around the wheels, putting eight-foot metal "sand ladders" in front of the tires, and watching the truck go a few feet before getting bogged down again. Over and over we dug him out in heat that was easily over 100 degrees. I couldn't believe that we were spending so much time helping a professional driver who should have known better than to drive where he was. To make matters worse, while the rest of us took turns digging and moving the sand ladders, the French girls sat chatting and laughing on a small dune. The Italian couple had a picnic.

After moving the truck maybe a hundred feet in more than an hour, I started feeling very dizzy and dehydrated. Foolishly I had finished my water midmorning. This is impossible, I kept thinking, getting grumpier by the minute. We could be here for days. Why doesn't he just radio his company to send a desert tow truck or something?

But even when the others were clearly discouraged too, including the Algerian driver who looked very worried, Henri was
unfazed. He kept up a steady stream of commentary in French,
Flemish, and English, grabbing our shovels and digging furiously if
someone slowed down. "You can never pass someone in trouble in
the Sahara. It's the golden rule of the desert," he kept repeating as
if reading my mind. "We will get this bastard out! Don't worry, just
a little more. There it is. No problem. Next time he's free. On va!
Easy on the gas. We are getting there." A few times the truck went
fifteen or thirty feet, even though the sand looked the same. And
sure enough, on one try that looked to me no different from the
others, he just started going.

"Don't stop," Henri yelled as the truck precariously picked up
speed on the sand, "don't stop. Go, go, go. Bonne route . . . Au
revoir." The sand had gotten just hard enough to hold the truck.
The driver looked very relieved but a little guilty as he headed off
toward the main track without stopping. We stood there exhausted and pleased that we had gotten the huge eighteen-
wheeler out. Henri lit a cigar and looked at our sand ladders lying
bent and mangled. One had been broken and ruined early on.
Another was bent at a perfect right angle so that half of it stuck
straight up. Even with four of us trying at once, we couldn't bend
it back. Henri paced and scratched his head, his hair sticking out
in every direction, muttering in Flemish. At Cristophe's suggestion we put the bent sand ladder on harder ground and drove his
station wagon over it until it was reasonably straight. By the time
we finished, the air had begun to cool a bit, but I didn't feel well
at all. I could tell that I had developed a fever, and my stomach
started cramping so badly that I had to limp a quarter mile away
behind a little hill to relieve myself.

When I got back in the car, I finally had to admit to Cristophe
that I needed some water. I had seen cases of mineral water among
the things piled in back, and all afternoon I had been hearing
some of the loose bottles bouncing around behind my seat. I

wanted to appear completely self-reliant so that they would be willing to take me along, but I knew that my pride would get me left by the side of the road dry heaving if I didn't do something soon. Cristophe just laughed when I finally asked him, generously offering me as much as I wanted. Flavored? With gas or without? I wanted to drink two whole bottles, but instead I just took a few swallows and offered the bottle to him. No thanks, he said, opening his own bottle — he'd rather have a flavored one. I cradled my bottle like a precious gift and though I tried to be restrained, sipping a little at a time, within twenty minutes I had finished more than half and was feeling a lot better. Cristophe got sleepy and let me take over driving for a while, but I hit so many bumps and we fell so far back from the others that he was soon wide awake and back behind the wheel. Even though we were going sixty miles an hour, it was not like driving on the interstate. Desert driving is a science, he told me, and it takes concentration and practice and quick reflexes to be able to drive fast on the piste without ruining the car. After that first taste, I couldn't wait to get back behind the wheel.

As the sun started to sink toward the horizon in the early evening, the landscape changed from flat to hilly. Then big, winding canyons appeared. Even deep in the Sahara there was every variation of desert landscape — flat gravelly places, deep canyons, soaring mesas and rolling, scrubby hills. As we followed the long shadows through a beautiful canyon, I felt pleasantly sunburned and sleepy and satisfied. I leaned out the window to take a picture of the cars lined up in front of us as we went around a curve. The wind was cool in my hair, the sun warm on my face. Then Cristophe hit a bump and I almost went flying out the window. I jumped back in and we laughed so hard that he almost had to stop the car. Both of us, I knew, were feeling the same thing — the great, giddy freedom of the desert that is like nothing else. To be in that huge space in our little cars was like being in the middle of the ocean in a tiny boat. And having the security of being with the Belgians — with their food and water, spare parts, Cristophe's knowledge of cars and Henri's knowledge of the desert — made it all feel like the great adventure I had been hoping for. Just fun and beautiful and exciting.

The shadows grew longer and plants began to appear as we approached the dry, semi-oasis village of Arak. First there were little, wiry bushes, then scraggly trees, then a whole eucalyptus grove. It was thrilling to see the green leaves among all the tans and browns, and to smell the cool vegetation in the air. Soon we could also smell a fire and when we went around the bend, a little adobe saloon came into view on one side of the road and a few small shacks on the other side. We pulled into the dirt yard of the saloon and Henri began negotiating with an old man over the price of gas, while the rest of us went inside to get drinks.

Inside it was dark and smoky. Years of grease and soot stuck to the walls and ceiling, and remnants of a thousand meals mixed into the dirt floor. The beverage offerings had now dwindled to a choice between beer, orange soda, and lemon-lime, all nearly warm in an old cooler. I drank two sodas before I even asked the price and was shocked when I found out that they were over a dollar each, twice what I had paid the day before and three times the price in Oran. An old, hunched woman told us they were serving omelets and fried potatoes for dinner, but when we decided to stay, there was not enough for everyone and she had to kill a chicken to round out the meal. We were there for three hours drinking beer and eating and telling stories. Sometimes everyone would talk in Flemish and sometimes in French so that I could understand a little. Cristophe was tired from all of the driving and Henri was very agitated over the price of the gas and the relative ease of the day's journey. "It's too easy," he kept saying, "Now the Sahara is like taking a picnic."

But wealthy Ludo was thrilled, opening beers for everyone, smoking his cigars. He loved the rustic café with its frontier feel and he kept saying, "This is why I came!" His English, it turned

out, was better than I had realized and he took an interest in my
story, wondering where I was from and where I was going. Every
once in a while he would translate part of their conversation into
English for me. And at one point he turned to me and announced,
"You will come with us until Tamanrasset." It was two days away,
and he confided to me that there was a good chance I could take
over driving the girls' car when they flew back from there. I had
already been contemplating the possibility, but to have things actually unfolding as I had hoped felt wonderful. The eggs tasted as
good as any I'd ever had and the beer was so strong that it immediately made everything hazy. I could feel my fever burning lightly
as I sat back and watched the candlelight flicker off the walls,
lighting up the happy faces of my new traveling companions.

DESERT FEVER

WE CAMPED THAT NIGHT in the desert a mile from the saloon and then, at Ludo's suggestion, went back in the morning for fresh omelets and bitter coffee. I felt revived by a deep night's sleep and as we all jumped in the cars and revved up the engines after breakfast, it was wonderful not to have to go foraging for a ride. As we went south, the terrain became sandier and prettier in its stark yellowness, but it was harder to breathe because of the fine dust in the air. As the sun got higher my fever came back, gnawing at my sense of well-being. Henri was excited all morning and whenever we stopped, he would say something about the "marabout hut" and the "sacred temple." In the early afternoon he waved his arm, signaling everyone to slow down. As we came over a small rise a grouping of sand-colored buildings appeared on the right side of the road, barely visible in the desert. In the middle of the grounds was the Marabou temple, a mosque founded by the hermit Moulay Hassan. It was a square adobe building with a conical dome in the middle formed by sticks which stuck out of the top, teepeelike. Inside, the floor was dirt but well kept, with three goatskin rugs and a lone, paneless window facing east. The other small buildings housed the current marabou, his family, and a few followers with their goats and chickens.

"For good luck, everyone who crosses the desert circles the temple twice for each member of their party," Henri announced with great ceremony. "Be sure to count correctly or we will have disaster." We had eight in our group driving five cars, so we each made sixteen circles around the temple. The track was so well worn that some of the curves were banking and everyone but Henri started driving fast. Chasing each other around the oval, it felt like we were in some kind of fairground derby. The marabout's wiry-haired, amber-skinned kids jumped up and down and ran back and forth cheering and adding to the commotion. Henri chatted briefly with the marabout and Ludo threw the kids some candy before we drove off honking.

When it was time to camp, we pulled a bit off the main track and parked the cars in a circle like an old wagon train. Only Ludo and I had tents. Henri, Cristophe, and the Italians slept in their cars, which required them to unload half of their gear each night. The French girls crawled into their sleeping bags next to their car but by morning they were back inside, impossible to wake up. A few times I tried to make small talk with them, but they would pretend not to understand my French. They preferred to stay to themselves, making jokes about Henri and the others. I didn't figure out until later, when I knew him a little better, that Henri had probably alienated them by making inappropriate advances. He was always making little comments and trying to put his arm around them. As the de facto leader, Henri seemed to want nominal respect from the group, but the French women gave him little, sometimes even counteracting his wishes when they had a chance to. If he said no stopping until dinner, they would pull over an hour later to switch drivers and take pictures. If he stopped to talk with other travelers, they would stay in the car, revving their engine every few minutes. At times over the next few days I felt the same way, not wanting to be constantly dragged along by him or held up by one of his frequent dalliances. But I couldn't say much of anything. Like the Italians, I was only a fringe member of the group. At night, I watched with envy as they all cooked delicious-looking meals while I ate sardines and rice, the only food I had left.

We got to Tamanrasset on December 31, the morning of my fourth day with the Belgians. Even though it had taken twice as long as they had expected, Henri was still complaining that it had been too easy, that there were too many tourists and too much paved road. "It is like driving the autobahn now," he said with disgust, "soon people will be coming on bicycle." I didn't have the heart to tell him that I had seen a group of people in Morocco who were biking and running from Paris to Dakar.

In Tamanrasset, the farthest city south in Algeria and one of the most remote cities in the world until the airport opened there in 1968, there were a surprising number of tourists — at least compared to the previous days out on the piste. Kiffiyah-clad Europeans zipped around in jeeps loaded with spare tires and extra gas cans. In a strange collision of old and new, goatskin canteens, made from whole goats sewn up at one end and tied at the neck, hung on the sides of the Land Cruisers and Range Rovers. At first, I thought these people had been goat hunting in the nearby mountains and canyons, but my Belgian friends told me that the slow evaporation through the goat hair kept water cool for days. It was a technique that had been used in the Sahara for ages, and though I was quite pleased with our flavored Evian, I was also tempted to "go native" and buy a goatskin to hang from my car when I took over driving.

I also wanted a kiffiyah to wrap around my head and a long cassock to wear, like the locals. I had a feeling that my fever might have been caused by all the fine dust I had been breathing and a good kiffiyah would keep it out of my hair and nose. And I had the same envy that I always get in Texas or Oklahoma or Wyoming, watching the locals strolling around in their big hats and Wranglers, with their pointed boots and huge belt buckles: when you are there, you want to fit in.

When we got into town I hoped to do a little shopping and sightseeing, and I couldn't wait to celebrate New Year's with a shower, a nice meal, and a room with a bed. Tamanrasset was a quiet tourist and trading town, with some stores and a few small hotels and restaurants. Nearby there were mountains that occasionally got snow, and spectacular canyonlands. Beyond Tamanrasset to the south there was only open desert until the border post, nearly a week away by car.

When we rolled into town, the Italians headed immediately for the nicest hotel, only partially expressing their appreciation for Henri and Cristophe's help. Now that they were safe they seemed embarrassed and self-important. Instead of driving back, they said, they would fly home and make arrangements for their car to be sold in Tamanrasset or driven back by someone else. The French girls went straight to the only youth hostel in town and said goodbye without any great ceremony. They seemed relieved to be rid of the car and able to get back on their own vacation schedule. They were going to tour the nearby mountains and canyons for a few days and then fly back to their au pair jobs in northern France. I was glad to see them go because they hadn't been much fun and I couldn't wait to take their car.

I was surprised when, instead of ceremoniously passing over the keys, Cristophe told me that Henri was not sure if we were staying the night and that he was going to try to sell my car (as I was already calling it) in Tamanrasset. The idea of not staying was more aggravating to me than the idea of selling the car. Even though the desert was very clean, I felt grimy from the days of perspiration and the layers of fine sand in my clothes and hair. I wanted to walk around a bit and enjoy the city, but if I didn't at least get a shower, I knew that I would become unhinged. I couldn't even imagine the possibility of going another week in the desert without one.

I felt a strong urge to tell Henri off, to just stay in Tamanrasset until I was ready to cover the last and toughest stretch of the Sahara. My fever was bad each evening, and I felt a strange kind of agitation from the heat and from having my schedule tied to Henri's every whim. In every direction I could see the desert beyond the town. Even in the east, where the mountains rose up, there was desert in the foreground. I had begun to be aware of the weight of the desert around me — the vast distances of nothing but dirt and sand for thousands of miles in every direction. I realized that as we went further south I had been feeling not only freedom in the desert but a kind of weight and claustrophobia that seemed as much physical as psychological. As I saw the wildness in the eyes of others around town, I wondered if perhaps my fever was a kind of desert fever, more from the place itself than any kind of microbe I might have picked up along the way.

I ate lunch with the others and kept quiet. Then I went with them to a local mission where Henri delivered boxes of bandages, vitamins, and medications to the nuns. He had stayed with them before and they seemed to be quite amused by him. He also tried to sell them my car and some of the numerous engine parts they had brought along. They laughed at the car because it was so small and ill-suited to their rough surroundings, but they did trade some gasoline for a few spare parts to an old Peugeot that he had sold them years before. And they gave us a big bag of dates and a can of pecans. Goods had become much more available in Tamanrasset in recent years, they told him. With the daily flights from Algiers, and the route north getting better, they were not so isolated any more. Henri grumbled about this progress, but the nuns seemed to take it all in stride. With or without the encroachment of the modern world, their work taking care of the sick was basically the same.

Before we left them we went into their small chapel. It was a single adobe room with light streaming in through one window and a simple cross on the wall. A young Algerian boy sat on a bench beneath the window studying a book. He smiled and watched us as we took pictures and said a few prayers. In that cool building, the weight of the desert was momentarily absent and everyone seemed to feel serene and happy. It was like being inside a big clay pot and for those few moments I relished the comfort of the walls around me.

Back outside in the bright sun, Henri moved us quickly into action. He tried to sell the car at three garages the nuns had suggested, but the prices were all too low, even for the parts. "Okay, now we go," he said, irritated when he came out of the last one, a tin shack at the end of the dusty main road. "So, you are the driver to Niamey?" he asked me, "You can handle this car?"

"Great," I said, "no problem, but I need a shower before we go."

"No time for a shower," Henri said, "We must get our permission stamps to go into the big desert."

I stood my ground and argued him into letting me take a shower. It would have taken him a lot longer to find another driver. Cristophe and Ludo were shocked by my stubbornness, but they ended up showering also, all of us paying to go into the public bathhouse. Afterward they were so happy that they kept thanking me for insisting on it. "I didn't realize how much I needed that!" Ludo kept saying, "I feel like I have new skin." When Henri saw us all clean-shaven and happy, I think he must have regretted not taking one himself. But to him, a shower in the Sahara made as much sense as an asphalt road.

In the early afternoon we pulled out of town towards the south, Henri leading in his blue Peugeot wagon covered with yellow racing decals, Ludo in his little green Renault V (infamous in the U.S. as "Le Car"), me in a white, two-door version of the same, and Cristophe following in his white Peugeot wagon. As we drove down the few miles of paved road toward the desert again, I was thrilled. The shower had revived me. Now I knew that I was going to make it across to sub-Saharan Africa. And I was going to have fun doing it.

THE LEADER, THE MECHANIC, THE COOK, AND THE AMERICAN

About five miles south of Tamanrasset we came to a roadblock with a small hut on one side. Some soldiers dressed in tan fatigues came out and asked for our papers. They recorded our names and passport numbers in a huge ledger and asked us to sign a paper saying that we had read the warnings and were aware of the dangers of driving further to the south. Henri tried to joke with them and schmooze, as if he were practicing for the greedy police and soldiers we expected to find in Niger. They were very stern and seemed to dismiss him as another foolish tourist. They obviously disliked being stationed in such a remote place, and they probably couldn't imagine why any sane person would voluntarily go farther. Four signs outside had the same message printed in Arabic, French, German, and English:

THE WALI OF TAMANRASSET COMMUNICATES:

Tourists travelling across the Great South should,
OBLIGATORY solicit the civil protection service
for a journey authorization.

BESIDES IT IS RECOMMENDED TO TOURISTS:

• To drive robuste vehicules in perfect state, well
equipped with special tires for these particular roads
and a filter against sand (oil bath).
• To drive in daylight in groups of at least two vehicules.
• To have extra food of two days in addition to their
need, a reserve of fuel, a medical first aid case and a
sufficient reserve of drinkable water.
• To never leave the main road and in case of breakdown, never get far from the vehicles.

Another sign had the death toll for 1987 and the just-posted
for 1988: 132 and 28 respectively. It had been a good year.

"Do we have special oil filters?" I asked Cristophe, just to make
sure. He shook his head, no. I knew we didn't have special tires.

"We have Cristophe," Ludo said, "we don't need the filters." I
counted the remaining water bottles and tried to calculate the
spare fuel for at least eight days of driving with only one more gas
depot. We seemed to have plenty of each, but who could tell? I
could only trust that Henri really knew what he was doing.

By the time we got our permits and moved beyond the barrier
it was late afternoon. The ground was very flat and we sped along
at seventy and eighty miles an hour, flying through sandy patches
without even slowing down. "The trick is to speed up for the soft
sand," Henri told us. Driving so fast, I had to concentrate on the
road in front of me, watching for rocks or ruts or ditches as
Cristophe had instructed me, making minor adjustments con-

stantly, like a race car driver. It was wonderful. At first I was a bit nervous, especially when I slammed the little car through a few jarring ruts, but in no time my eyes got sharper and my reflexes seemed to quicken.

In the evening we stopped on a hard-packed plain so flat that the earth seemed to be curving around us. Everyone was exhilarated. There had been some fun driving before Tamanrasset, but not like this. We had not seen one other car all afternoon and no one had gotten stuck in the sand or even been bothered by difficult tracks. Ludo announced that he was going to prepare a gourmet dinner for New Year's Eve and everyone pulled out bottles of beer and scotch and champagne that had been saved for the occasion. I started digging through my bag to see if there was anything I could contribute, but Ludo stopped me.

"From now on you eat our food," he said. "You are now on our team — the Belgique Expédition Sahara! You must learn to speak Flemish of course."

As the sun was setting, we ate a four-course meal and drank the champagne, some wine and beer, and the scotch. We built a small campfire as the stars began to come out and rolled down the windows on Ludo's car and played tapes of Mozart and Tchaikovsky and then later some '70s Belgian disco. Ludo led a series of toasts, "to our fearless leader, Henri," "to the most expert mechanic in the Sahara, Cristophe," "to the American!" And we toasted him back, "to Ludo, the best chef from Algiers to Niamey!" It was a perfect night out in the crisp desert air, and even Henri seemed to be glad to have me along. For the rest of the trip Ludo loved to toast "the leader, the mechanic, the cook, and the American." As the American on the expedition my job was to be tough, naively optimistic, and whenever necessary, overly brash to officials.

Ludo insisted on doing the dishes himself and I could see the end of his cigar lighting up as he hummed along with the music. As the last orange light was dying in the west we could see a truck driving along the edge of the horizon, seeming to follow the earth's curve. Just as we noticed it, it changed its course and began coming toward us, headlights growing as it came. Fifteen minutes later a beat-up old truck stopped near our campsite, loaded with people and possessions. In it were twenty or thirty Africans — four or five in the cab and the rest sitting in the open back. They seemed to be sitting on piles of foam mattresses and various bundles of goods, with other bundles hanging from the wood railings around them. I figured that they were poor nomads or scavengers of some sort, riding about the desert collecting things. Henri spoke to the driver and found out that it was a kind of bus service taking some Nigeroise migrant workers home to Niger with their accumulated wealth from the north. They had detoured when they saw our fire, to make sure that we were okay.

Ludo spoke to a couple of the men in the back and the whole crowd laughed when his words were translated. Some of the kids climbed up on the rails, craning their necks to see us and our gear. Cristophe ran to his car to get a big bag of candy while the truck sputtered and Henri stood on the running board asking about the road ahead. We gave peppermint sticks and hard fruit candies to the kids and then to the adults too. Ludo also gave them a few of the beers and half a bottle of champagne. "Happy New Year," we told them, "Bon Année!"

"Bon Année!" they yelled back, clearly amused by our high spirits. As they drove off, we stood waving in a line and they waved back until they went out of sight into the darkness. In spite of the cold that night, I left the cover off of my tent so I could see the stars through the open screen roof. It was a beautiful night, and the stars seemed to swirl all around me. I lay awake a long time feeling very grateful and very lucky, my fever only slightly burning. When I finally went to sleep I dreamed again about my childhood friends — endless, joyous, exhausting dreams that left me almost breathless when I woke up. I don't often remember my dreams, but in the desert they were so vibrant that I always did.

Throughout the mornings I would mull them over and mix their colors and strange movements into the stark scenery around me, almost dreaming again as I drove.

On New Year's Day we drove fast for a couple of hours until the terrain began to change and the route became unclear. We stopped frequently and Henri would climb up some rocks or stand on top of the car to search for a direction marker. He would scan the surroundings until he saw some rocks piled up or the carcass of an old car. "There it is!" he would yell and we would speed off in that direction. The further south we got, the further apart these markers seemed to be.

The car and truck carcasses that we passed were eerie and ominous. Sometimes they would have a placard next to them telling the story of the people who had perished in them. When the cars were found, Henri told us, they were usually burned up and the people were dead somewhere nearby. People who lost their way in the desert would panic and light their cars on fire to attract attention and then huddle nearby waiting for someone to come help them. Often they were found just a few kilometers from the main track. The army would tow the cars to the main route so that others could use them to guide their way. Because of the low humidity, they wouldn't even rust and some of them were twenty or thirty years old, completely stripped of every usable part. When we passed them I would always look closely to see what kind of car it was and then find myself imagining its history as I drove along. The long sedans were always African gold runners or immigrant smugglers on their way to the coast. The burned out VW buses were from bungled hippie caravans in the early '70s, surrounded in their last moments by panicked flower children. The big trucks had carried lone Algerian soldiers who slumped on a dusty hill as their trucks burned.

"Many tears have been cried in this sand," Henri said earnestly. "If you get lost, you have a ninety-nine percent chance of surviving if you can keep your head. Most people can't keep their heads."

In the afternoon on New Year's Day, we began crossing an area called the Dunes of Alooney that Henri called one of the most treacherous places in the Sahara. There was soft sand everywhere and many small hills with cliffs that were hard to see. Our pace slowed considerably. At times all four cars got stuck and we had to dig them out one by one. Other times Henri would stop and walk around a bit, searching the horizon. Then he would announce that we had been going the wrong way and would have to go back over the ground we had just painstakingly covered.

Toward evening the wind kicked up a heavy sandstorm making it impossible to see where we were going. The sand blew in waves so that sometimes visibility was a few hundred yards and sometimes it was only a few feet. Above us the sky turned dark gray and black so that I could look right at the round disk of the sun and not blink at all. "Drive slowly so that you don't go off a cliff!" Henri screamed at each of us, but soon we were stuck in soft sand so that we couldn't move at all.

Henri appeared next to my window with the hood of his Eskimo parka pulled forward as far as possible. "Just stay in your car!" he shouted, "I am going to look around." And then he disappeared into the blinding sand. I shut my windows as tight as I could but the sand still blew in, piling up on the floor and seats. Sometimes I could see Cristophe leaning back in his seat, napping with his hands behind his head, and Ludo chewing on a cigar, bobbing his head to the music he was playing. But for a while the wind blew so hard that I couldn't see at all and it was as if I were alone inside a tornado spinning around and around.

I tried to read a bit but couldn't concentrate, so I wrote a little in my journal, musing about the strange noises outside and commenting on Henri's passion for the desert. As the howling symphony of wind played around me, I thought about the fact that everyone should have something that they are passionate about, something that elevates their life above mundane experience. "In all things, it is the passion that gives the meaning," I wrote, wondering as I wrote it what Henri could possibly be doing out there and how he would ever find his way back to the cars.

Forty-five minutes later, with the winds beginning to subside a little, Henri returned. "It is clearing," he yelled, "I think we are on the right track. I found some markers not too far from here." We heard a rumbling through the haze and to my astonishment a caravan of three cars and two motorcycles went by, not fifty feet from us. Henri waved to them that we were okay and then tried to signal them to turn to the left, but they seemed to just keep going straight.

"They are going the wrong way," he said, his eyes flashing. A chill ran down my spine as I realized that I didn't really have much reason to trust his judgment. Sure he had been across the Sahara before, but he was beginning to seem alarmingly unstable. After Henri talked to the others, Ludo looked over at me, raised his eyebrows and shrugged. When things quieted down and we were digging out I asked Ludo if he thought we should try to catch up with the others. He said he would prefer it, but Henri would hear none of it.

"They are fools," he yelled loudly, as he paced back and forth with his hood still on. "I won't follow them off a cliff." For two tense hours we inched along until we came to the end of a long canyon, walled on three sides.

"It is the wrong way, we'll have to go back in the morning," Henri announced without apology. The rest of us were furious, but Henri seemed almost pleased, exploring caves while Ludo cooked dinner and Cristophe worked on the cars. I had the eerie notion that he was purposely getting us lost just to make the trip more challenging. I checked with Ludo to see how much food we had left.

"Plenty, plenty," he said, "We will need gas long before we need food."

At dinner, Henri ate noisily, slurping at his noodles and every bit of the sauce. The rest of us were tired and quiet, though occasionally Ludo tried to make to lighten the mood with his dry humor. "It was a very good storm today," he said, "I think Kevin was worried when the sand blew in his car. I saw him writing a death letter."

The next morning it was clear again and Henri seemed more settled. For three days we had beautiful driving, flying over open spaces that seemed more pure and serene than the previous days. Getting lost or getting stuck or breaking down became such a part of the daily rhythm that it didn't even seem inconvenient after a while.

Though we were all driving carefully, the suspensions and drive axles began to fall apart because of all the jarring ruts. Whenever a car had trouble, Cristophe would crawl underneath or get under the hood and fix it faster than seemed possible. When Ludo's whole drive shaft started dragging on the ground we were all pretty worried, but Cristophe rigged some straps through the doors and underneath to hold it in place. The only problem was that Ludo's doors wouldn't close properly because of the straps, and after a few hours of driving he would emerge from his car cov-ered with sand. It wasn't long before three out of the four cars, in-cluding mine, were rigged the same way.

On the morning of January 5, we got up and left before sunrise, hoping to make a good 150 miles to the border post at In-Guezzam. The terrain was perfectly flat in every direction, without any dunes or hills or any kind of vegetation. The horizon was curving all around us so that it was like driving on a craterless moon, or on top of a big cueball with some dirt and gravel on the surface. As the sun came up, we spotted a Tuareg camel caravan camped off to the east. Despite Cristophe's and my objections, we drove toward them, parked a short distance away, and walked over.

Six men sat around a small fire drinking tea while their camels lounged nearby. They were cordial, but not enthusiastic until Henri tried to say a few things to them in Arabic. They were amused by his attempts and from the gestures, I think he may have suggested trading a car for one of their camels. They offered us tea and we brought out some bread that they were obviously pleased to have. They didn't look straight at us, and didn't seem to feel any particular need to talk as we sat with them. I couldn't tell if they were shepherds, traders, or bandits, but they told us they were traveling from west to east across the Sahara, a feat I could barely imagine. We sat on the windy plain with them and watched the sun come up as we drank mint tea and listened to the camels baying. Then we got up, took a few pictures, and left them to their journey.

We got to In-Guezzam late in the afternoon, our first town in five days. It was an ugly military outpost with rows of aluminum sheds that served as both homes and stores. Army trucks were everywhere, and a few tanks were parked in the streets and in fenced-in compounds. As we approached the main street, we could see and hear all kinds of commotion, with soldiers yelling and people hurrying back and forth. A dozen big trucks were lined up on the wide street, and nearly a thousand dark-skinned Africans were being forced into them. The Africans looked ragged and very scared and soldiers carrying machine guns kept shouting instructions while the truck engines roared and groaned.

After the quiet of the desert, it was such a noisy, crazy scene that we could scarcely believe it was real. I couldn't tell exactly what was going on, but it was obvious that it was not an everyday occurrence. So while Henri went off to buy gas, I got out my camera and began taking pictures. Through the lens the scene began to look much more real. I could see the faces of the mothers clutching their children, the slumped shoulders of the young men, the angry eyes of the Algerian soldiers. When I took a picture of one particularly agitated soldier, I immediately knew that I had made a mistake. As the shutter clicked I saw his eyes looking right at me and in a second he was tugging at my camera, demanding that I give it to him. I tried to refuse, but completely lost my French, just stammering and clutching my camera. When he started yelling and pointing his gun at me, Ludo stepped between us with his hands raised and quietly talked him into taking only the roll of film and leaving me with the camera. Anger welled up inside me — at the fear and the harshness of the scene, at the arrogance of the soldiers' authority. The roll had almost all of my Saharan pictures on it. Before I handed it over, I regained my French enough to get my passport taken away also. Everything escalated so quickly and so unreasonably that I couldn't make sense of it — Ludo telling me to be quiet, the soldier yelling at me. I wasn't even sure what I had said. I tried to back things up and talk him out of taking my passport, but he wouldn't yield. Only then did I realize that he was the lieutenant in charge of the other soldiers. He announced that we could not cross the border there and that we would have to go back to Algiers to get a new passport.

Cristophe and Ludo were not pleased. When Henri came back he was furious, and he started ranting and raving in Flemish. He wanted to leave me there to deal with it. Then he tried to bribe the soldier into giving my passport back, which resulted in his passport getting confiscated as well. We could go back to Algiers or go deal with the captain at the border post, the lieutenant finally told us after ten minutes of wrangling.

"Our American!" Ludo said sarcastically as Henri glowered at me. I felt awful. I didn't think they could send us all the way back to Algiers, but just having the thought in our minds depressed all of us.

At the border checkpoint, we had to wait two hours until a soldier from town showed up with our passports. But the captain seemed fair and told us not to worry. He said that the soldiers were very edgy because they had been dealing with these illegal Nigeroise refugees for weeks. It was not so much a problem that I had photographed the deportations, he said, it was just that pictures weren't allowed anywhere around the town because it was a military post. He was very smooth, but obviously lying.

A French couple who were waiting for their exit stamps told us that the Nigeroise refugees were remnants of the famine migrations of 1985. Thousands had fled north to Algeria from Niger and Mali when crops throughout the Sahel had failed, and now the government had decided to round them all up and deport them because unemployment was causing unrest among the Algerians and they didn't want them there any longer. Trucks packed with hundreds of people standing shoulder to shoulder, all their worldly belongings hanging on the sides, was not an image that the Algerian government would want the world to see.

While we were waiting, the refugee trucks began coming slowly toward the border, some of the deportees just walking along behind them. I loaded another role of film in my camera and shot a few pictures upside down from behind the car door. Ludo caught me and laughed uproariously, "Vrai Americain," he kept saying, "Incroyable!"

"We can't go through all this and not get the shot," I said. "It's a matter of justice." He loved that, but he made me put the camera away and said he would tell Henri unless I promised to give him copies of the pictures.

When we finally got our passports back, the confiscated roll of film was not with them. The captain was very nice about it — they would develop the film to make sure there were no shots of military installations, and then they would send the photos to me. I gave him my address, feeling naively hopeful that maybe the whole scene would just end up saving me development and postage costs.

By the time we got our exit stamps, the sun was starting to set. We made sure we drove far enough to get beyond the actual borderline, which was fifteen miles further south, and camped out in limbo between Algeria and Niger. Rather than celebrating, everyone was quiet and wrung out from the day. Even Cristophe, who was a very gentle soul, seemed pretty mad at me about the whole experience.

In the morning we had more officials to contend with. We were surprised to find almost a dozen other travelers waiting at the

Niger border post. There was no sign of the refugee trucks and Ludo said that he had heard them during the night heading south-west, away from our track. The border guards finally got things going around nine o'clock, insisting that everyone open up their cars and their bags for inspection. Three Nigeroise soldiers wandered around, ostensibly doing a customs check, but looking more like they were shopping. When they got to me they wanted to know what my small camping stove was and whether I wanted to give it to them. I had promised the Belgians that I would be good from then on, but I was not about to give away my stove. I was firm, but I tried to keep it light.

"Non, non. C'est necessaire pour moi," I told them smiling. "C'est petite, mais c'est necessaire." Ludo and Henri quickly distracted two of them while the other one went through my bag. He seemed pretty disappointed with my meager goods and when I offered him a box of matches he took them and moved on in disgust. Ludo tried to give them a bottle of wine, but they were Muslims and they were not interested. To my relief, they ended up leaving us for easier pickings with the wealthy-looking British couple nearby.

We had to wait in line in the hot sun outside the ramshackle customs building for another hour to get our passports stamped. When I was finally near the front of the line, a man showed up carrying a large, barbecued slab of meat with a long tail still on it. He cut pieces off for each of the men sitting around the office, weighing each in his hand and then charging them accordingly. For the man behind the desk he cut a large piece and didn't charge him at all. Both Ludo and I were sure that it was a dog's leg, but Henri said that it was a goat and had a piece himself.

We drove hard for the next two days, anxious now to get to Arlit, the official end of the desert and the beginning of sub-Saharan Africa. At lunchtime on our second day in Niger, in the middle of nowhere, we came upon the tiny mission town of Tchizorine. As we drove down the single street, I was amazed to see little trees and rocky garden plots and children running out to greet us. Most of them were an exact combination of Arab and African features, with partially kinky hair, tan skin, and large eyes. While Henri went into the schoolhouse to deliver a bag full of medicines to the missionary, the kids crowded around us asking for "un cadeau" or "un stylo." I didn't know what they meant until Ludo and Cristophe pulled out a fistful of pens they had brought for just such an occasion. The kids loved it, and they got even more excited when candy was brought out. When I tried to take a picture of them standing by a tree, everyone wanted to be in front so badly that before I could snap the picture, some of them had crowded right up under the lens and I could only get them from the eyes up.

As we were heading back to our cars, almost fleeing the commotion we had caused, I saw a young man sitting alone by a wall with elegant, colorful, hand-carved statues of gazelles and camels set out for sale. With their proud, elongated lines and muted colors, they seemed to capture all of the loneliness, tenacity, and serenity of life on the edge of the desert. They were so strikingly beautiful after all the time I had spent in the barren desert that I could not resist buying a couple. As we drove along afterward through miles and miles of barren landscape, I put the camel and gazelle on the seat next to me, feeling haunted by the smiling faces and hopeful eyes of the kids we had seen so far from the rest of the world. They seemed so poor and isolated that I wished we could have done more than give them a few pens, some medicines, and a few dollars for statues. When I mentioned this later, Henri laughed heartily. "That was a good village," he said. "Soon you will see more poverty than that."

All afternoon we drove fast across a flat, rocky rise, knowing that the town of Arlit was out there, soon to peek over the horizon and signal an end to our desert journey. There were still no trees and no grass, no sign of animal life, just the warm wind blowing through the windows as we went. Towards evening, with the sun starting to sink to the horizon behind us, the town finally appeared, almost dead ahead. I had to blink to make sure it was real. I wanted to floor the gas pedal, drive up to a hotel, run straight into a shower, and then stretch out across a big bed. But instead, Henri eased to a stop and the four of us got out and took some photos of the cars: all beat up, a last dune behind them, the orange light on our faces as we sat proudly on the hoods. Ludo opened a bottle of warm champagne and we all drank a little and toasted each other and the cars, pouring a few splashes over the bumpers. Then we drove casually for the last twelve miles, savoring our last few moments in the great, wide open space.

THE SAHEL

Indeed he knows not how to know who knows not also how to un-know.
SIR RICHARD FRANCIS BURTON

FRONTIER BANQUET

THOUGH MY FEVER WAS UP again as we drove into Arlit, I was looking forward to a celebration. We could feel the excitement just driving down the street. It was a true frontier town, a frenetic outpost that served not only as a welcome center for those just across the Sahara, but also as a watering hole for the engineers and laborers who manned the uranium mines in the desert to the northeast. The dusty main street was lined intermittently with shops, empty lots, and a few ramshackle hotels. Africans, Arabs, and a smattering of Europeans crisscrossed the streets. Crowds gathered around grills made from old oil drums on which men were cooking meat kabobs and skinny chickens. These vendors yelled to us as we went by and other locals yelled about buying auto parts and selling auto parts and gasoline and parking our cars in a safe place and helping us find a good hotel.

Henri stopped to talk to one of these pitchmen and while we were waiting a small crowd formed around my car. Soon I could see nothing but dirty T-shirts, dark limbs, and eager faces. I rolled down the window and said, "Bonsoir." Before I finished the word, three young heads were squeezing through the window, looking around the car.

"Whoa, whoa," I said, holding up my hand as one of them bumped his head against mine, "Non, non. Excusez-mois, s'il vous plâit." To my amazement, they eased back out, smiling, firing questions at me faster than I could hear them.

"Ça va? Ça va, monsieur? Cadeau?" they were all saying, not seeming to know what the words meant. When I responded, they would just repeat the questions, smiling and wild-eyed. I felt like I was playing a game without knowing the rules, but no one seemed to mind. After five minutes of confusion, the crowd parted and I could see the other cars pulling off. Ludo smiled and shrugged and waved for me to follow. We circled around the town again and then followed a man into a parking lot behind a two-story hotel that had balconies along the front and sheets hanging out the back. It looked like something out of the old French Quarter in New Orleans.

Henri began discussing business with some of the many local car merchants while we walked around the streets, scouting the market for food and money-changers, and checking for news about the road ahead. Every time we passed a brochette stand, Ludo and Cristophe would buy a stick of grilled chicken or goat. It smelled wonderful, but I wouldn't try one because I was too worried that the meat might be bad. One of the books I had read recommended not eating any meat in Africa that you hadn't seen alive. I thought it sounded like a wise precaution to follow. For the rest of the evening I watched to see if Ludo and Cristophe would show any signs of imminent demise.

When we found Henri back at the cars, he was grumbling about the low parts prices. "The market is gone, there are too many cars crossing now," he said. "But prices are always the lowest in Arlit." He hadn't had success selling any of the spare parts, but he had arranged a big dinner for all of us upstairs at the hotel — a celebratory banquet that would include some Germans he had met. It seemed he had already begun celebrating. His face was flushed and his breath smelled of whiskey. As he headed back into the bar, it was obvious that our showers would have to wait, but we didn't mind.

We put on our best clothes and washed up at the cars with the bottled water. We got Henri and headed up to the banquet room, a dark place decorated with worn red velvet curtains and peeling, gold trim. The table was set with a variety of mismatched plates and glasses and everything was lit by two oil lamps on the wall and a few candles on the table. In our state of sensory deprivation it all looked very nice. In the subdued light it felt like we were in an Agatha Christie play, and there was a subtly villainous air about the room that added to the excitement. Between drinks I kept imagining the oil lamps catching the velvet curtains on fire or one of the waiters pulling out a knife to assassinate a spy at our table.

I drank too much too fast. We had champagne and beer, toasting each other and the Germans while we ate a first course of cheese-and-potato omelets. Before the omelets were finished a jovial Nigeroise came in with two women, one dark and heavyset, the other thin and lighter-skinned. He introduced them as his sisters and began shaking hands all around. Henri gave him a grand welcome and I thought he was an old friend until the man made a little presentation for the crowd, telling us about the attributes of each of his sisters and asking whether we liked them. He acted like a gypsy selling flowers in a restaurant, except that he wasn't selling flowers. I couldn't understand the whole speech, but Henri kept clapping his hands together in delight and everyone else was laughing nervously. I understood though, when he said we could sleep with one or both if we wanted, or two of us with one, or take a hot bath, or anything else that might give us comfort and pleasure.

Henri grabbed at each of them, pulling them onto his lap and patting their rear ends. Cristophe laughed shyly, but I could see that Ludo was angry at the interruption and at Henri's distasteful behavior. I was simply horrified that this man was pimping for his sisters and I couldn't stop watching their faces, thinking that he was actually their brother and wondering what they were feeling in such an awkward situation. The skinny one looked scared and uncomfortable. The fat one looked bored and indifferent.

Ludo pointedly asked the man to come back after we were done eating and the jovial pimp said, "Yes, good, later." And then he sat down with the women and joined our meal as the main course of chicken and goat meat was served. There was plenty of food, and after the talking started up again, their presence just made the party more festive. The beer was very strong and before long the whole scene was hazy. There were lots of small groups talking around the big table in various languages and I had trouble following the conversations. I became so drunk that I began to worry that we were being drugged so that the African waiters who were circling the room could pick our pockets. I shared my theory with Ludo and he laughed so loud that everyone stopped talking to hear what he was laughing about. When everyone else laughed too, I decided I'd better slow down on the beer.

The more that Ludo and Cristophe drank, the more they talked about the comforts of home that were awaiting their return from Niamey in a week or so. Cristophe could not wait to get back under the cars in his garage and get back to work on the new addition he was building on his house.

"Won't it be too cold for building?" I asked.

"No, no," Cristophe said, "after the Sahara, I welcome the cold. For me, cold is good."

Ludo wanted to get back to his wife and his fire and his leather armchair and his cats. They both said they couldn't believe I was really just beginning my trip in Africa, that I had a couple more months ahead of me, and that I was planning another whole journey in Asia after that. I couldn't believe it either, but I told them that I was excited to get on to see my Peace Corps friend Dave in Timbuktu and to explore sub-Saharan Africa — the true Africa in my mind. Already Niger was noticeably different from Algeria. The people had much darker skin, were much more gregarious, and seemed much more needy. If I didn't have my Belgian friends to translate for me, and the security of their car, I probably would have been petrified to be stepping into the Sahel. I was excited about the new world unrolling in front of me, but I also felt envious of Ludo and Cristophe for being able to go home soon.

Sipping my beer, I couldn't help but wonder about the fact that every time I reached a milestone, I was beset by urges to go home. Now that I was in the Sahel, a place I'd wanted to see for a long time, I felt a little anxious about going further, starting something new and foreign all over again. "Okay, you made it," the voice seemed to say, "now go on home, comfort awaits." I couldn't blame Ludo and Cristophe for thinking about home and talking about home. I wanted that comfort too. After nearly three months of traveling, I would have loved some rest and relaxation in my own world. But I knew it wasn't going to happen for a long while. "I'll be gone at least eight months, maybe a year and a half," I had told everyone before leaving. The Sahara seemed like a long road to leave behind, but for me it was really just the beginning.

When we were nearly finished with dinner, another man came in with three more women, but the jovial pimp chased them away before Henri even had a chance to grab one of them. The heavy whore had already attached herself to him and although he wasn't entirely thrilled with her, she clearly did not seem inclined to let him get away. Under the table she was making clumsy efforts to endear herself. Henri responded by drinking more and laughing louder and making so many abrasive attempts at humor that pretty soon even the pimp did not want to talk to him.

I made the mistake of looking too long at the skinny girl as she sat staring at the tablecloth. She looked innocent and sad and I was wondering how she had gotten to this place. She looked up and saw me watching and made herself come over to sit next to me. I was a little embarrassed, but I tried to be nice while the whole roomed swirled around me. In fragmented French, she asked me if I would like a hot bath and made it clear that I could have a hot bath and a warm bed and other things for very little money. I asked how much for only the bath and she said that it was the same as a bath with all the rest, about fifteen dollars. Somehow, a fifteen-dollar hot bath didn't sound too crazy. Before coming up to dinner we had discovered that the hotel was pretty expensive. Even Ludo didn't want to stay there, and he and Cristophe, now that they were really drunk, encouraged me to go with the girl, saying that they were going to sleep in the cars and watch the gear.

When the bill came it was much more than anyone had expected. The Germans were angry and the whole party broke up in a hurry. The next thing I knew I was stumbling along a side street with the girl, going to see about the hot bath and trying to watch the route so that I could get back afterward. She led me into a long hut that seemed to be made out of cinder blocks, with a corrugated aluminum roof. There were little rooms inside without doors and I thought I heard some people sleeping at the far end. Most of the rooms were empty except for small sleeping palettes on the floor, the blankets and pillows looking worn and unclean. She led me to a cubbyhole at the near end and lit a lantern. To my surprise, there was a comfortable-looking bed with lots of pillows, and there were mudcloth fabrics hanging on the walls. She sat me down on the bed and tried to remove my shoes.

"Where is the bath?" I asked. I hadn't seen one and unless it looked really great, I wasn't planning on taking anything off.

"Demain matin," she said. "Tomorrow morning. Maintenant, restis. Restis." She patted the bed, looking nervous and worried that I would not stay. But it was clear that she would be staying too. I thought about how long I'd been without sex, and how long I would probably keep going without it as I traveled, and then I looked at her sitting there nervously. Somehow it seemed as though it would be meaner to her to just leave. I figured that I should stay, as a "life experience," but as the seconds ticked by, I just couldn't — not there, in a shack without a door, and a jovial pimp lurking nearby. Except for her big eyes, I didn't find her at all attractive, and somehow I sensed that sleeping with her would probably wipe out all that I had gained in the desert, the bit of strength and clarity and tranquillity that I had felt growing inside me.

She cried when I left, and outside I felt awful and scared as I tried to find my way back to the main street. I had sobered up considerably and everything seemed much sharper, including the danger of being alone in such a place in the middle of the night. I passed only one person walking back — and he looked like the pimp, though it was so dark I couldn't tell for sure. I didn't stop, even when he paused, and I was too frightened to even look back, holding my breath as I tried to listen for him coming up behind me. When I turned onto the main street and stole a glance backward, I could see that he had turned and headed on his way.

I found the parking lot, but no one was guarding the cars at all. Ludo and Cristophe were not in theirs, nor was Henri. I climbed inside my little Renault V and fell asleep with my head on the arm rest and my back against the steering wheel. I woke several times during the night to strange dreams and noises and joint cramps, but I could not really pull myself awake until well after sunrise when I heard shrill yelling and screaming in the street nearby.

Blinking, I could see Henri in the middle of the street, his face flushed and his hair disheveled. The pimp and the heavy prostitute were there too, taking turns yelling at him, first one, then the other, backing him down the street. The woman was screaming bloody murder, looking more like a bully than a victim. The pimp was not jovial anymore. He was calm and menacing, his words punctuated by an occasional rise in volume. The essence of what he was saying was clear — he wanted more money. "Tip" was the main word that was being batted back and forth, and even in my sleepy, hungover state, I could see that the reason the prices had been so low was that a high "pourboire" was expected. Fifteen dollars for the night and then fifty dollars in the morning. Intimidation seemed to be part of the routine, but Henri was compounding the problem by lying and insulting her, insisting that she wasn't worth a tip and that she was a fat pig and that he hadn't even slept with her.

Ludo and Cristophe showed up in the middle of the scene, freshly showered and shaved. Cristophe got a tire iron out and put it on top of his car within easy reach, and the three of us fussed around our cars and kept an eye on the combatants until they finally settled on twenty dollars, an amount that seemed to leave everyone feeling cheated. Seeing Henri's face, I was very relieved that I hadn't stayed for the hot bath. And Ludo and Cristophe were almost as mad as Henri. They had been so drunk that they paid sixty dollars for a buggy room at a hotel down the street. At least they had gotten showers. I began my trip through the Sahel still wearing the yellow dust and dirt of the Sahara.

CHANGE OF PACE

AS WE BEGAN OUR JOURNEY towards Niamey, the all-day drive from Arlit to Agadez was quiet. The landscape along the worn dirt track was still arid and sparsely populated. At midday we passed a Tuareg in fine, light-blue robes and a white turban riding alone on a small black horse. His face was wrapped against the blowing sand. Later we passed a boy, eleven or twelve years old, riding proudly on a huge camel, spurring it into a gallop as we went by. Neither of them looked our way as we slowed to watch them. Gradually, as the day went on, a few plants began to appear, scraggly bushes and twisted trees that to our sensory-deprived eyes seemed beautiful in the surrounding dust.

Driving into the big town of Agadez early in the evening was nearly as exciting as driving into Arlit the night before. There were cars and trucks and women and children and traders moving through a maze of streets. Just like Timbuktu in Mali, Agadez was an ancient trading town that served as the center of trans-Saharan trade for the people of a huge region now covered by Niger and Nigeria. But unlike Timbuktu, Agadez has remained a big market town. It was once known for its slave and gold trade but it is now famous for the Tuareg silversmiths who make traditional jewelry and saddle decorations along with a growing number of trinkets for the tourists. And because of the uranium mines, the French have built a paved road all the way from Agadez to the capital in Niamey. Where Arlit seemed to be a depot for the men who worked in the mines, Agadez appeared to be the transport center for the companies that ran them. From Agadez, it was possible to drive the more than five hundred miles to Niamey entirely on a paved road.

At dinner that night everyone was pretty quiet and it was clear that something had changed. Henri was depressed about the previous night and sure that he now had AIDS. I didn't know until Ludo told me that reports had just come out saying that HIV was believed to be rampant among African prostitutes. Cristophe was even more quiet than usual as we ate, and when Henri started talking about taking an indirect route to Niamey through more desert, he put his foot down, saying he wanted to go directly to the capital on the paved road. Henri replied that he wanted to spend a few days in Agadez and then take a leisurely pace, looking for people to buy the cars and parts along the way.

While we were eating and talking, I kept hearing the sounds of engines revving across the town. During the day we had heard reports that the Paris-Dakar Rally would be in Agadez that night and after I was finished, I set out to find their camp. I didn't have to ask many times to find them. They were in a large, walled-in compound on the edge of town — hundreds of brightly colored cars and team trucks with crews decked out in matching jumpsuits full of their sponsors' logos. It was a gaudy scene, but thrilling after all the time in the desert, as if the modern world had found its way into an ancient time. African pop music was playing from a loud-speaker truck. Groups of men laughed and drank, while others huddled around their four-wheel-drive sport utility trucks trying to fix a broken part or tweak a tired engine. To my surprise, nearly every jeep running the race was a Mitsubishi Montero, though the two specially-built Peugeot wagons, as was customary, held a huge lead on all the others. The Peugeot team, I was told, had a private camp elsewhere.

No one gave me even a scrutinizing look as I wandered the camp at will, checking out the different trucks, looking over people's shoulders while they worked, talking to a few of the men. Each crew, I found out, had three drivers and every team was re-quired to have at least one follow truck — a big transport truck with plenty of spare parts, specially outfitted with huge desert tires, and a crew of five mechanics including at least one African. To participate in the two-and-a-half-week race cost an average of $120,000. Usually they ran the trucks and motorcycles from Paris to Malaga, Spain, and then over to Morocco and through Algeria along roughly the same route I had come. This year, though, be-cause of criticism by the Algerian government, they had run from Paris to Marseilles and then over to Libya to run the desert entirely there. It had been brutal on the trucks, but most of the people had loved the wildness of the Libyan desert. Because of restrictions against travel in Libya, no Americans could participate.

"There is nothing there but oil wells and sand," one Dutch man who was racing on his motorcycle told me.

"And the army," his friend added.

"Oh yes. And the army."

Peugeot had reportedly spent a million dollars on each of their two station wagons. There seemed to be some annoyance and jeal-ousy that they were both a day and a half ahead of the next closest drivers. There were only five days left in the race, heading straight west from Agadez, across the northern edge of the Sahel, to Senegal. The Peugeot team had five follow trucks and a full-time design crew that worked year-round improving their car. They had won so many times that it wasn't really even a race any more, and there was talk of putting technical restrictions on the participants, as they do for the sailboats in the America's Cup, so that it would become a driver's race again.

Of course most of the people were in it for the adventure and the camaraderie anyway. The whole affair was seen by many critics not as a race, but as a decadent frolic by wealthy, insensitive Europeans through one of the poorest parts of the world. The requirement to put one African on each crew had been initiated two years before in response to criticism that the race did nothing for the Africans but endanger their lives. Every year, a Peace Corps volunteer told me later, people were killed during the race — sometimes participants, but more often African villagers who were in the way when the cars or follow trucks came racing through their towns. That year no one had been hurt yet, but they were just starting their route west through the much more populated area of the Sahel. I watched the African mechanics working expertly under the cars and shuttling back and forth to the big trucks for tools and parts. I saw their pride, and the adoration on the faces of the small local boys following them. Was this token compensation for the intrusive spectacle that the race imposed on the Africans? Or was it good sport and good business all the way around? As all of the trucks roared to life the next morning, the noise alone was enough to make the whole enterprise questionable.

That night, though, it was just a big party. I felt like I was with a circus crew or in an army camp on the eve of a campaign. When people started lining up for dinner, I got in line too.

"Steak or chicken?" the white-jacketed chef behind a large grill asked.

"Chicken, please," I answered in French, waiting for someone to pull me from the line.

"One or two?" he asked.

"Two, thanks," I responded, unable to stop myself. Then I got a carton of chocolate milk and some orange juice and sat down in the middle of the party. I watched the ten- and twelve-year-old African boys running around as I ate my second dinner of the night, and my third. It was exhilarating and revolting all at once, and I couldn't help but enjoy it. I had been thirsting for the comfort of the familiar, and it was delivered as if dropped from the sky, all the seductive excess of modern culture stopping for one night only, right in the middle of the most foreign place I'd ever been. If I could have, I would have gladly traveled with the caravan for a few days.

I returned to our campsite feeling happy and a little ashamed at my overindulgence. I could tell immediately that things had come to a head. Henri was banging about by his car, unloading and rearranging things. Car parts were strewn all over the ground, shining in the moonlight. I had not realized that we were carrying so many. I was excited to tell everyone what I had seen, but Henri's demeanor warned me away. He was entirely deflated, looking tired and old and much smaller than usual. I could see that his hands were shaking.

I veered off towards my car to set up my tent for the night. Ludo came over.

"Cristophe and I have decided to go straight on to Niamey tomorrow and fly home as soon as we can get a plane," he said.

At first I thought it meant that we would all be rushing to Niamey, which I didn't mind too much. I was already weeks behind my planned arrival date for Timbuktu. But then I realized that they were going to leave me with Henri and go on by themselves.

"We will take my car and you and Henri will take yours and the white Peugeot," he said.

"What about Henri's car?" I asked. It was our emblematic car — painted blue and yellow and covered with racing decals.

"We sold it tonight," he said, without any expression of relief. "Henri is upset though. We have made him do it for less than he

wanted. They would only take that car because they liked the racing stickers."

I didn't know what to say. Things had changed so quickly.

"We had to have some of our investment back before leaving," Ludo said apologetically. "Who knows? I am not sure I will
see any of the rest."

Much of the trip Ludo had been excited about the large prof-
its they were going to make selling the cars in Africa. But then the
cars started falling apart, taking too much of a beating in the ruts
and the sandstorms, and he had become less committed to his "vacation with profit." It was all Cristophe could do to keep them
running in one piece. But Henri kept insisting that the cars would
fetch great sums.

"They don't care if they are running or not!" he would pro-
claim. "If they are broken we can also sell the parts to fix them. I've
seen Africans make cars work with soup cans and coat hangers."

Even when faced with the low prices in Arlit and Agadez,
Henri had kept this up, insisting the market would be better further down the road. "We'll go to Ghana," he had said. "In 1978 I
sold a Citroen in Ghana for six times what it cost me in
Marseilles, plus enough marijuana to fill two suitcases. And it
would only run in second gear."

But Ludo and Cristophe had finally run out of patience with
Henri's bossiness and unrealistic boasts. In the desert they had
been very respectful of his desire to be the expedition leader. More
than once they had talked of possibly going on to Ghana with
him. But now they had clearly changed their minds. They'd had
enough physical adventure and they did not have the emotional
energy for another odyssey on the last five hundred miles to
Niamey. They wanted to get home to their families and friends, to
the colorful scenery and quicker tempo of their own country. We
were all feeling emptied out from the rigorous deprivation of the
desert, in need of physical and emotional rejuvenation. Watching
Henri pulling the equipment out of his car and pacing around

among the piles, I could not help but wonder if perhaps he had been in the desert too many times, if perhaps he had been emptied out too many times over the years without ever being refilled.

And now I would be alone with him for five days or a week or two weeks. I felt a little betrayed by the others and disappointed that our team was splitting up. But when I thought about it that night, I knew that it was wrong for me to be anything but thankful for the way they'd treated me. I had been extremely lucky to get such a great ride through the desert. Even with Ludo and Cristophe gone, it was still a pretty posh situation — free food, free gas, my own car to drive and an experienced, albeit shaky, guide. When the cars were gone I would be all alone again, and I was happy to have a few more days to prepare myself for that.

In the morning I said good-bye to Ludo and Cristophe. Ludo hugged me three different times. Cristophe shook my hand twice. They told me to give all the gendarmes hell and to take care of Henri if he got too crazy. Henri, for his part, was cordial. He too had decided that things would work fine with the new plan. Cristophe had tuned up all the cars as best he could and he and Ludo were going to leave their car with a friend of Henri's in the capital. If we didn't sell one of the remaining two along the way, Henri would sell all three when we got to Niamey. We promised to get together in Belgium some time, or in the States, and I told them that most of all, I would miss their great company.

"Bon voyage!" Ludo yelled as he drove off, chomping on an unlit cigar.

THE HEART OF WEST AFRICA

FOR SIX DAYS HENRI and I moved slowly towards Niamey, trying to sell car parts along the way. In every town Henri seemed to know some strange and disreputable character — usually a European who had crossed the vague line between native and foreigner. Though most of them would probably have been in jail if they had stayed in France or Belgium or Germany, here they lived like petty lords. "Come to Africa, be a king," seemed to be their motto. Though there were few fences anywhere in Niger, these expatriates always had big gates, full-time guards, and cook/maids rushing around their three-room homes. They all held a condescending view of the Africans that at times was outright disdain. "You can't trust them to do anything right the first time," they would say, or, "They have no concept of time. A day is a minute to them." These shop owners and tradesmen and black marketeers would greet Henri as a comrade-in-arms and then try to maneuver and exploit him in the most amicable way. They all seemed to have the same deep corruption and loneliness that he had, and they would take him in as kin for a few hours and then be glad to send him on his way.

I sat in on some of these meetings, but often I would just roam around the town a bit, or watch the cars as I read or wrote under some tree. Whenever we stopped in a village, kids would appear. They would crowd around my car so that I could barely open the door. And then they would follow me wherever I went asking for "gifts."

"Monsieur, cadeau! Cadeau!" they would yell, holding out their hands to me and to Henri.

"I'm famous all over Africa," Henri joked. "Everywhere I go they call out to me. But they all think my name is Mister Cadeau."

It soon became clear to me that most of the west Africans saw Europeans primarily as people they could get something from. Centuries of trinkets had created an unhealthy relationship that made it almost impossible for people from two different cultures to have any meaningful interaction. Though the locals were often very pleasant about it, the goal was almost always the same — get something before the white man leaves. Almost everyone I'd pass would say, "Ça va? Ça va bien, monsieur?" In France this means, "How's it going?" — just a casual greeting. In francophone Africa, it seems to mean, "Would you like to start a conversation that will lead to a gift for me?" When I didn't answer, the locals would just keep asking, sometimes belligerently. When I did answer, they would then ask where I was going, where I was from, how many children I had . . . etc. Then after a pleasant conversation, they would start looking to see if I had anything with me they might want. That was the pleasant approach in the villages. The other approach along the well-traveled tourist tracks was simply mob and grab. Sometimes I couldn't even get out of the car.

At first I rebelled against the whole system, not wanting to play a part in reinforcing a negative dynamic. I went out in the

streets with no money at all and let the kids dig through my pockets and run through their whole list of questions, trying to joke
with them until they would finally settle down. Then I would ask
them some questions about themselves. Sometimes they would tell
me about their school or show me a toy that they had made from
pieces of scrap metal. In the northeast, near Agadez, some of the
kids played a kind of hackey-sack game, kicking a rolled-up wad of
trash around a circle. A few times I joined them and left them all
giggling because I couldn't kick it as well as the smallest of them.

But even these brief, enjoyable encounters would invariably
be broken up by a group of older kids who would send the younger
ones scurrying and then start in with the "cadeau" routine all over
again. Sometimes they would push a friend forward who was crip-
pled or who had a bad cut that was festering horribly.

"You must go to the hospital," I would say emphatically, and
they would all giggle.

"I have no money for the hospital," one boy with a deeply lac-
erated leg told me one day, smiling and holding out his hand while
flies crawled around his wound. He and his friends would not tell
me where the nearest hospital was or what it would cost to go
there. I went back to the car, got some money for him, and tried
to get him to promise to use it to go to a doctor. He nodded emphatically. But when I gave him the bills, the whole crowd
mobbed him and the money was divided everywhere, leaving the
injured boy with almost nothing. I watched in frustration as some
of the bills were ripped into small pieces and could only hope that
they might eventually be reassembled. This happened again and
again in villages along the road. I finally had to turn my back on
even the injured kids, but then I felt worse than ever. It was impossible to give and it was impossible not to give.

After just a few days in sub-Saharan Africa I felt like this was
my tortuous African koan. Every dime meant a lot to most of the
locals and a dollar or five dollars was a major windfall. Knowing
that I had a few thousand dollars saved in my bank account for the

trip, I felt I should be giving away something. But then I would be just another in a long line of white people who came through, gave handouts and went away. Henri felt that he had a perfectly equitable solution. He would give them candies and old pens that he had brought along to hand out.

"I think they are past the pen stage," I told him one day when I was feeling particularly frustrated with the whole situation, "maybe you should give them some paper."

The poverty just seemed too pervasive for anything to really help — anything short of regular rainfall. The Sahel, I came to realize, is a region entirely on the edge. It is on the edge of the Sahara and it receives just enough rain in a good year for the local people to eke out a meager farming existence. When the rains don't come, it is devastating; if they don't come for two or three years, there is widespread famine. Most of the region has much less vegetation than most of the southwest United States, looking like what most Americans consider to be desert. After four weeks in the Sahara, though, it seemed almost abundant. As we drove along, we were amazed by all of the vegetation — more bushes and trees, an occasional garden, even a few patches of green grass here and there. I was soon told that it had been a very good year for rain, well above average.

Driving down the narrow tarmac road, I could glimpse some of the quiet patterns of the local life. There were clusters of huts, with thatched roofs and thinly covered sides through which I could see a woman nursing her child or a man sleeping in the middle of the day. Sometimes there were herds of goats with young boys watching nearby. And sometimes there were women pounding cassava roots into meal with large wooden poles. The *harmattan* — a warm wind that blows dust in from the Sahara all winter — had started blowing, and though I couldn't really see the fine sand in the air, I could see it in the people's hair, and feel it in my sinuses. Every evening, because of the dust, the sun would turn into a glowing orange ball long before it settled to the horizon.

At night we would try to camp well outside of the towns so we would not attract attention. Invariably though, the people would appear, sometimes hours after we set up camp. They would sit just outside the firelight and watch every move we made. With Ludo gone, I had taken over as the cook and I was usually too busy to really notice our visitors while I was preparing the meal. Henri would eat voraciously and loudly, but between his noises, I could hear men breathing beyond the firelight and sense the hunger and sadness. It would fill me with guilt and anger. I was hungry, but I knew they were hungry too. Their gray turbans and long robes would move closer and closer into the firelight and then almost next to us until eventually they would ask for something.

"Don't give them anything," Henri would say, "or we'll have a hundred in the morning." But in the morning when we could see their kind faces, he would often give them something before we left.

One night, when Henry went straight to bed after dinner, I offered the leftovers to three kids who had been watching us for a couple of hours.

"Non, merci," a little girl who looked about ten or eleven years old replied. The two younger boys with her shifted. They were shivering a little from the cold, so I motioned for them to come closer. She smiled and moved in to warm her feet and hands on the fire, pulling her nine-year-old brother with her. A smaller boy who might have been five or six stayed just out of the light for a little while, but eventually he came in and sat right beside me. The girl had big, curious eyes, a small upturned nose and an angelic voice that sounded like she was singing when she talked. "C'est jolie ça!" she would say, tilting her head back and forth when I showed them something they were particularly curious about. They wouldn't take any food or tea because they had already eaten, she said, but I finally talked them into sharing some chocolate with me. They told me that their father was the policeman in the nearby town and that they lived in the closest house to our campsite. We could see a light burning about a mile away.

Even though it was already late, we talked by the fire for nearly an hour, all in French, with her and her brother correcting me when I made a grammatical error. They told me about going to school and playing soccer, and about life in their village. They said that in years before, people had been very hungry, but that now it had rained for three years and the life was very good.

"The cows and goats have much milk," they said, "The gardens are very big."

I asked them if they had seen the Paris-Dakar Rally because I knew it had passed nearby and I wanted to know what they thought of it. The little boy took a deep breath and his sister told me they had not seen it, but they had heard it roar by when they were in school. And then later they heard that one of the motorcycles had hit a small child on the road. At first I thought I had misunderstood, but I hadn't. They said that a three year-old in their village had been killed by one of the racers. The mother of the child had been so distraught that something had happened to her as well, but I could not understand exactly what. The kids were very matter-of-fact about all of it, but they were also wide-eyed in the telling and I knew that they were rattled by the whole thing.

No wonder no one else has come out to the camp, I thought as I poked at the fire, wishing I could really talk to the kids, that I could offer them some adequate explanation. But there was nothing I could say, because I couldn't make the roaring trucks and the quiet African town fit together myself.

After a while I knew I should turn in, so I showed them how my tent went up. Each of the two poles snapped together with the help of their internal bungee cords and then they formed the front and back arches that made the whole thing nearly stand up on its own. The kids loved it and couldn't wait to get inside. I didn't have the heart to tell them no. The four of us climbed on in and the littlest boy fell asleep on top of my down sleeping bag, while I showed his brother and sister some postcards I had bought in

Europe with pictures of Paris, Venice, and Rome, and my maps of Africa showing all the terrain in color with big swatches of yellow for the desert and green for the jungles. They knew almost every capital when I named a country, but they had never seen them on a map. They were particularly excited to see where their home was, right in the heart of West Africa. They scoured the area nearby to find names of places that they knew, and they seemed very surprised that Niamey was so close and that the great Niger River went through other countries besides their own.

"C'est jolie, ça! C'est très jolie!" the little girl said with a big smile before she dragged her brothers home.

I slept peacefully all night and in the morning I woke to Henri yelling, "Allez, allez — go away!" I could see my three little friends, scampering across the sand back towards their house. I yelled to them before they got too far and they came back, though the littlest brother kept giving Henri a wary eye. Henri tried to give them bread to make up for his rudeness, but they politely refused. Instead, the little girl brought out three small oranges and gave them to me, "for breakfast." Then the older boy produced a leather bracelet with cowry shells and some small, colorful beads sewn on it. It was a "friendship bracelet" his sister explained as he smiled broadly.

I let them help me pack up the cars, though Henri was sure they would steal something. I just laughed at him. Before we left I told the little girl that she was "tres jolie" and that they were all very good kids.

"Merci, monsieur," she said with her big smile.

"Merci, monsieur," the older brother said also, while the little one smiled. Then they picked up their bags and headed off to school. Only later did I realize that I hadn't given them any "cadeau" in return and they had never asked.

THE BIG VILLAGE

WE GOT TO NIAMEY on the morning of January 12. It was the biggest city I'd been in since Oran, and my first real African city. There were stoplights and traffic circles and road signs, but it was a quiet town and it seemed to me more like a sleepy suburb than a national capital. Henri had held together surprisingly well after Ludo and Cristophe left, and he had been almost pleasant company at times. We went straight to the post office and found seven letters waiting for me, including two that had a bunch of Christmas cards from my friends. I felt like I had won the lottery.

We checked into the main tourist hotel, a so-called luxury hotel that could have gotten only one or two stars in Europe. In Niger, it was a four-star hotel. It had a swimming pool and hot showers, and Henri figured that we could find some good prospects for selling the cars there. I was just happy that we had made it all the way to Niamey without selling my car, because I had been dreading the prospect of riding with Henri, putting up with him smoking and talking incessantly all day. Now he wanted to share a hotel room to save money. At first I said no, but when I calculated how much it would cost — four times my daily budget at nearly forty dollars a night — I had to accept.

When we got to the room, he immediately insisted on taking the first shower. Since he hadn't taken one the whole month I was with him, I didn't object. I was worried that if he didn't do it then, he might get distracted and go another month. I put on a pair of running shorts and went out by the pool with my mail. Even though it was winter, the midday sun was very hot and a dozen Europeans were lying around the pool reading and napping under the palm trees. I felt tired and hot and burnt out on the strange surroundings of Niger, so it was wonderful to be at a place that seemed more like Florida than West Africa.

I first read a letter from my Mom talking about Christmas, what everyone had done back home in Virginia and how strange it was not to have me there. I reread it three times, savoring every detail of the food they had eaten, the card games they had played, the presents they exchanged. They had saved my presents in a small pile next to the tree and toasted me at dinner while my chair sat empty.

When I was folding the letter carefully back into the envelope, I heard someone nearby speaking French and it took me a few seconds to remember where I was. The men around the pool were wearing Eurobriefs. Lizards were sleeping on the rocks between the weeds nearby. A maid was walking down the sidewalk with a pile of towels, her skin the color of ebony and her hair light brown from the dust of the *harmattan*.

I dove into the water and felt absorbed by its slippery coolness. The heat and dust were dissolved and carried away for a few moments. I closed my eyes and let myself float deep down, imagining for a little while longer the Christmas I had missed. I got out and

read a letter from my sister and one from my grandparents, saying
how strange it was to have me so far away and how they didn't really understand why I wanted to be in Africa, but that they hoped
the trip was going all right.

I noticed that a man next to me kept staring, and when I
stared back he asked me in heavily accented English if I had just
arrived. Then he told me that no one usually swam in the pool because the water was questionable.

"You have not swallowed any have you?" he asked.

"I don't think so," I answered. In fact, I had tried not to, but
after he said something, I could taste it in my mouth, and feel a
few drops sitting in my ears.

"That is good," he said, "But perhaps you will take a hot
shower when you go inside, just to be safe."

I moped back to the room thinking I was already feeling a
little queasy. The room was a disaster area. There were puddles on
the bathroom floor and a trail of towels to one of the beds where
Henri was asleep, stark naked and snoring like it was the middle
of the night.

I got into the shower and tried to think about my next move.
Earlier in the week I had promised Henri that I would stay two
nights in Niamey to help him with the cars and to see if they
would need to be driven to Ghana. In my anxiety over losing the
car, I had been thinking that I would possibly skip Timbuktu and
keep on with him if he did head further south. Now I could feel
that it was time to move on. A ride all the way to Ghana would
be nice, but I had been planning to go to Timbuktu — in the opposite direction — since I had first conceived of the trip. Having
come so far to get to the Niger River, I was not yet ready to follow
it south to the coast. I wanted to follow it north, upstream into
Mali as it reached back into the Sahara and then turned southwest toward the capital at Bamako. As far as I knew, Dave was still
in Timbuktu, and even though it was kind of impractical to head
that way, I wanted to go there. Timbuktu, in my mind, was a grand

destination, a place that beckoned on its own, justifying almost any effort to reach it. And to speak English again with someone I knew, to really hold a conversation, would be wonderful.

While Henri slept, I set off in the afternoon heat to look around the city and find out about transportation north. I was hoping I might be able to take a boat, but I soon found out that the river was too low from Niamey to Timbuktu early in the year. I found two regular bus services to Gao though, the first big town in Mali, about halfway up river. Gao was the ending point of the north-south route that I had not taken through the Sahara. From there I was sure that I would be able to hitch a ride with someone the last couple hundred miles. The only catch was that the daily bus service from Niamey was run by a private firm that had windowless, broken-down buses filled beyond capacity. The government bus service went just three times a week and cost twice as much, but it had windows and sold "only as many tickets as seats."

I walked around the city, looking for the Niger River and trying to get a sense of life in the capital. When I finally found the river, it was narrow and brown, with steep, tree-lined banks. I watched for a while from a bridge as shirtless, sinewy men washed clothes in the muddy water. They had piles of pants, shirts, and sheets on the rocks near the shore and they worked hard scouring every inch of each piece with soap bricks. Then they banged the clothes against large, flat rocks to get the soapy water out before rinsing them again. It was laborious work and I could not help but wonder if the clothes or the men could take many of these washings.

Nearby on the banks overlooking the river were embassies and some of the nicer homes of the city, most of them surrounded by trees and bushes and high gates. They were nearly invisible from the street in front, where the locals were selling peanuts or trinkets or standing around listening to the first matches of the all-important wrestling season on the radio. Amazingly, when I walked by these men and the boys hanging out with them, most of them didn't seem to notice me. They were so busy listening to the wrestling matches, and so used to Westerners, that they didn't even try to sell me anything, let alone get a "cadeau" out of me.

I found the national zoo with its small collection of animals, remarkable mostly because nearly all of them had long ago disappeared from the Sahel. It was sad to see giraffes and buffalo and zebras once plentiful in the region now caged in twos and threes. With a little more grass and a few more trees in the Sahel, I could easily imagine them roaming over the vast, empty land I had driven through between Agadez and Niamey. Drought, hunting, and especially deforestation had eventually made the land too precarious for them. Now only the humans were able to hang on, and a lot of them just barely.

On a street nearby I found a local market bustling with the Saturday crowd. Men, women, and children bought and sold and traded what looked like a vast array of colorful goods. I soon realized that the same things were sold in each of the many booths. There were just three different patterns of brightly colored African cloth — blue and yellow, green and gold, and best of all, bright red, with cartoonlike medallions of the new president, Ali Saibou, printed in gold. I could recognize these patterns on many of the women I saw, presumably the year's style. The men sometimes wore long tunics of local cloth. But more often they were dressed in secondhand Western clothes that had been shipped over by one of the aid organizations. Since getting out of the Sahara, I had seen men and kids in some crazy clothes — Little League T-shirts from Ohio, gas station uniforms with the names still sewn on, black-and-white referee shirts. But in the market in Niamey I saw the best outfit yet — a tall, cocky young man who was a blackmarket money trader, in a pink and white maternity shirt with "Baby in Here ⇩" printed on the front.

I bought a greasy beignet, some peanuts, and an orange Fanta and walked among the stalls. The sounds of African music competed with the wrestling matches squawking and echoing from radios all around. Besides the clothes, and a few vegetables, the locals were selling small cans of sweetened milk from Holland, cans of processed meat from Denmark that looked like Spam, and mackerel sardines from Japan. I bought one of each to keep in my pack as emergency food. Then I got another Fanta and headed back to the hotel.

I found Henri in the bar, drunk and fairly euphoric. He had already sold two of the cars and enough of the parts to allow him to go wherever he wanted with the remaining gear. The prices had not been as good as he had hoped, but what the hell, he said, neither was anything in Africa anymore. Maybe in Ghana things would be a little more like the old days. His drinking partner at the bar assured him that they would be, and they both lamented my having come to Africa too late to get in on the good years.

Sometime in the middle of the night Henri stumbled into the room, sounding as if he was breaking everything in his path. In the morning I found him on the floor and thought for a second that he might be dead. He wasn't. And when I woke him up he told me that he had just found it too difficult to sleep in the soft bed.

That night we had a nice dinner of chicken, potatoes, and onions in the hotel restaurant. I was already getting tired of the place, but it was great to eat a whole meal and Henri was so civilized that it was almost nice to be with him. He asked me about my plans for the first time, and we talked about the ironic beauty of the Sahara. "It is absolutely barren and still incredibly beautiful," he said. "It is boring and completely exciting at the same time." For a few moments I worried that he might change his mind and head to Timbuktu with me. But he also told me that this trip had tired him more than any of the others, and that he might wait a few years before doing it again. He was looking forward now to relaxing on the beaches of Ghana.

We said our "good-byes" that night, and well before dawn the next morning I put on my backpack and headed out to the bus station, walking through the quiet streets to the northwest edge of town.

NEW COUNTRY

I GOT TO THE BUS STATION three hours before the scheduled departure time but could not get a ticket on the government bus because the seats were all booked. I didn't want to ride the bus with no windows, so I decided to hitchhike. I walked out to the customs barricade on the northern edge of town and after an hour of waiting, the first vehicle to come along was the government bus. Bags and crates were tied on the roof in huge piles, and inside it was filled to capacity. The driver sold me a ticket though, for 30 percent above the regular price, and made room for me in the middle of the backseat where there were already five people sitting. The customs officials started going through the bags, and by the time we left nearly an hour and a half later, we had squeezed another person onto the back bench and seven or eight more on top of the bags and boxes in the aisle.

I was the only white guy on the bus, but I was not the only American. Sitting near the window three rows in front of me and across the aisle was an older black man. He was dressed in a new tunic made of blue-and-black African cloth with a matching hat. He was with two younger, smartly dressed Africans, but he stood out almost as much as I did. His skin was chestnut, considerably lighter than the ebony black of the locals, and his manner was more stilted, more self-conscious than any of the Africans. As we began bouncing over the dusty backcountry tracks, I could also see that he was considerably less comfortable with the accommodations.

When we stopped I made a point of saying hello to him, but he just said "hello" back and kept walking, like he wanted to pretend I wasn't there. I was thinking, Hey, somebody from home. But he clearly did not see me the same way. I overheard him talking about the locals as "my brothers," and "my people." He seemed surprised and almost indignant that I had shown up to invade his African experience.

As the day went on the air in the bus got hotter and dirtier, and lengthy police checks made it clear the trip was going to stretch well beyond the allotted twenty-four hours. At each police check everyone had to produce their papers and my passport would receive a full-page stamp with multiple signatures scribbled over the purple or red ink. The *harmattan* was blowing so badly that we had to keep the windows closed to keep the heavy dust out. It was easily 110 degrees in the back of the bus. We were all perspiring, practically suffocating in the thick air, and the endless jarring and bouncing over ruts was making everyone so nauseated that the frequent stops became a welcome relief.

By late afternoon, my compatriot was fed up and he began to seek me out during the stops to commiserate. He was a professor of African-American studies from Chicago, he told me, and this was his first trip to Africa. He said he considered it a homecoming. He had flown into Ghana to see some of the slave forts there

and he was going to see the Dogon country in Mali and some of
the other rural life of West Africa before flying out from Senegal.
"But my God," he said, "I didn't expect this!" He had never imagined that there would be dirt tracks between major towns, and
corrupt policemen, and buses without any ventilation.

"My old school bus was better than this," I said, trying to be
sympathetic.

"My school bus was better than this," he responded with a
meager smile, "and my school bus was *not* your school bus, I can
assure you."

We drove on the piste along the river, and as we got further
north it became more desertlike, the scenery more beautiful.
Women were pounding millet next to their mud huts and picking
cotton in sparse, windblown cotton fields. Men fished from long
pirogues — the local, handcarved canoes. Others mended nets
along the shore. These scenes were probably similar to those seen
by some of the first European explorers 190 years before as they
searched for Timbuktu. I glanced at the professor, but he was not
watching. His head was back, a piece of muslin over his face to
protect against the dust. I knew he was probably feeling the nau-
sea and sinus pain that I had suffered at first in the desert. I had
gotten used to it, but now the jarring roads and the odors of fifty
sweating people and a couple dozen chickens were making me feel
pretty nauseous too. It was a rough ride for my first day away from
the little Renault, and I wouldn't have wanted to try it at sixty
years old.

We reached the Niger border post at Ayorou around sunset,
pausing briefly to get our passports stamped. It was a peaceful place;
the river was so wide that it looked like a bay, and the orange sun
played off the small waves. People fished from the marshy shore,
and as we were boarding the bus to leave the local mullah began
calling out the evening prayers from a small mosque.

We got to the Mali border at Labbezanga around ten at night,
and it soon became evident that there would be problems. The

driver came out of the customs shed looking crestfallen. There were some whispers outside the bus and then the word went around that we would have to unpack again. They wanted to inspect everything. Some of the men who had brought goods from Niamey looked especially distressed — not so much because they had anything to hide, but because, I was told later by one of them, their profit would be cut substantially by bribes. For the rest of us it just meant delay.

As soon as it was announced that the inspection could not take place until morning, the women took out their pots and their hand-carved spoons and began meal preparations. As many people as could fit would be able to sleep in a warehouse nearby, we were told. I was politely offered a spot by one of the old men, but when I saw the dilapidated conditions inside the building, I decided to put my tent up outside instead. I was feeling whiplashed and exhausted and I knew the professor must have been feeling a lot worse. I went to look for him to invite him over for Spam and sardines and to offer a place in my tent if he needed it, but he was already in bed. His companions had found a room for him in one of the few buildings nearby, a little motel that had an earthen fireplace and used live tree branches as part of the roof. He had gone to sleep without even eating.

In the morning, when we all assembled at the bus at 7 AM, he was feeling better physically, but he was clearly frazzled. He had paid eighteen dollars for the room and the mattress had been dirty and uncomfortable. Then we had to wait three hours before the police even started their inspections. When they called him into the office and tried to charge a tariff for his camera, he came out furious. "These people are shameless," he said, "I can't believe that they are allowed to get away with it." I gathered that his companions had worked out some fee and I think that many of the others fared a lot worse. But the officials didn't bother me at all, even after I accidentally gave them the wrong passport. I was still using the extra one I had gotten for Algeria, and I thought it might really cause some problems when the Malian police realized I was traveling with two. But they didn't seem to mind at all.

Even in Africa, I had begun to realize, there is a strange kind of racism under which a white person often comes out ahead. Though people were always staring at me and talking about me and trying to get handouts from me, there was an implicit defer-ence in their attitudes that seemed to be a residual effect of the colonial era. In cafés and markets I would get served before the lo-cals, and even the policemen and bus drivers seemed especially ac-commodating to me. I would have thought that this could be attributed to my perceived status and relative wealth, but by that measure, the professor should have been treated better than me. It seemed sadly ironic that the Africans whom he saw as being more closely related to him because of their skin color than I was, saw him the same way and treated him accordingly.

When the bus finally pulled out near noon, the mood was resolutely glum. Only the women seemed untouched by it all, chatting and ignoring the men as usual. The track got better as we got closer to Gao, and the mood picked up a bit. We went through some interesting fishing villages, but the professor barely looked up, keeping his face covered to protect against the dust. He seemed to have given up on that portion of his trip. When we got to Gao at nine that night and the local police an-nounced that no bags could leave the bus until morning, I thought he was going to blow a gasket. His assistants found a place for him to stay for the night and whisked him away before he said anything to the police. Unsure whether my tent counted as a bag, I put it up right next to the bus, practically on the main street.

I woke up early the next morning and was taken through the police inspection quickly. It was Sunday, January 15. I found out that the professor had hired a car so that he could go west on the paved road that started just across the river. I had a thought that he might invite me along, but he didn't. I shook his hand through the window.

"Good luck with your travels," he said emphatically, "I hope the rest of your trip is better."

"You too," I said, feeling worried about him and sorry that we hadn't gotten a chance to talk more.

COMFORTABLE DATES

I HAD BEEN HEARING ABOUT GAO since I first found out that it was possible to drive across the Sahara. Gao is the southern end of the road for the second most traveled route through the desert, or the beginning of the road for tradesmen heading north. Because of its proximity to the river and the desert, and its strategic position near the center of West Africa, I expected it to be a bustling trading post. At least, I thought, it would be a wild, interesting town like Arlit or Agadez. Instead, it was just a tired little three-street town. Most of the buildings were made of cinder block with tin roofs. There was a small grocery store with half of its shelves empty, two ragged hotels that served food at outdoor tables along the dirt main street, and quite a few shops dedicated to car and truck parts and other miscellaneous hardware needed for running the desert. Teenage boys and grouchy old men sold gasoline here and there in large plastic cans.

I asked about travel to Timbuktu and was told that there might be something "tomorrow," so I got a coffee and an omelet at one of the hotels and sat outside to write letters and see who might drive up.

It wasn't long before two jeeps that had obviously just crossed the desert rolled into town. Then two others arrived with men who were working locally. None were going northwest along the river to Timbuktu as I wanted, but one of the Europeans who lived in town told me where to catch a truck heading out from Gao. They all stopped at the "truck yard" to pick up passengers for extra money, he said. Usually passengers just rode on top of the cargo, but sometimes the drivers would let you ride up front, especially if you were foreign and could pay some extra money. There were no buses in that direction, he told me, and still no boats because of the water levels.

A kid who had attached himself to me showed me around town while I checked in at the truck yard and stocked up on some food, including some pasta and a can of tomato sauce, along with the standard portions of rice. At the truck stop they said that there would be "beaucoup" trucks and bush-taxis leaving for Timbuktu in the morning. I paid twenty-four dollars for a ticket and then hiked three-and-a-half miles to the Camping Yantala tourists campground south of town. There I was able to shower and do a little reading and writing without being bothered by the locals.

In the morning I hiked back into the truck yard early to see what was waiting. The truck yard was a big, sandy, walled-in yard with a few old barrels lying around — and no trucks. When I asked the men in the little ticket office, they seemed annoyed.

"One truck is going to Timbuktu in this hour," the man said in French. I showed him my ticket and he nodded, "Okay, okay." Then he turned back to his discussion.

"Leaving in one hour?" I asked, "Today?"

"Yes, okay, okay." the man said angrily.

I sat down against the wall to read about the early explorers of Timbuktu. For a long time in the eighteenth and nineteenth centuries, the reputation of the city had grown in Europe, eventually taking on mythical proportions. Rumors from the trade routes had given rise to a common belief that Timbuktu was a city of enormous wealth, with doors and rooftops of gold. Arabs and Europeans would send cloth, spices, and other goods across the desert, and gold and slaves would come back in exchange. Timbuktu was the name most often associated with this desert trade, but long after the coastal regions of Africa had been explored by Europeans, none of them had found the fabled city. In the late 1700s and early 1800s a number of expeditions set out, but all of them met with disaster. In 1795 a Scottish doctor named Mungo Park and a handful of men spent a year negotiating difficult situations, including imprisonment. All of the men on his expedition had died of illness and hardship, and, still several hundred miles from the city, Park finally had to turn back in order to save himself. He achieved some fame in England when he told his story, and was sent back in 1804 with a couple of army units, plenty of gifts, and ample firepower. But this time he did not behave as humbly with the local tribes. Though they got within fifteen miles of Timbuktu, he and his men were ambushed on the river after shooting many natives and insulting a local king. I vowed to avoid similar mistakes, no matter how circumstances might tempt me.

After about an hour and a half of reading, not one vehicle had come but some people had started to gather on the other side of the yard. I waited a little while longer, staring at my ticket dolefully, and then asked the man in the booth. "One hour," he said.

I looked at my watch. "At three o'clock?" I asked pointing to the three on the dial.

The man nodded, again annoyed, "Yes, yes. No problem."

At 4:30 I asked again, angry now and wondering if I had been ripped off. I felt like an idiot for having paid him anything without a vehicle even being there. He looked at his watch, which I

now noticed was off by a few hours, and said, "Demain matin," —
tomorrow morning.

I argued feebly, but I'd had so long to think about it that I did-
n't put up much of a fight. If he had ripped me off, I figured I could
take it up with the police. There weren't a lot of places to hide in
Gao.

I crossed the yard to talk to some of the people who had come
in through the other gate carrying large bundles. They stared at me
all the way across and they were so inhospitable looking that I just
walked right out the gate. I hadn't gone two hundred yards before a
rusty old brown-and-yellow truck came lurching down the road past
me and into the compound. I went back, and sure enough, it was
the truck going to Timbuktu, piled high with bags of dates and already carrying seven people. The driver, not much older than I, was
too busy to speak to me directly, but one of his four assistants (or
"carboys" as they proudly called themselves) told me they would
pull out in fifteen minutes. I showed him my ticket, which seemed
to confuse him, but he soon came back and said it was okay.

We all climbed up on top of the dates, sat there for an hour
and then were asked to climb back down. The truck left with just
the driver and two of the carboys, then came back twenty minutes
later with more people and bundles on top. The rest of us loaded
up again. There were twelve passengers on top of the load. Half of
them lined the front edge so that they could brace their feet on
the roof of the cab. The rest of us found seats in the depressions
between the bags.

About an hour later, with the sun heading down, we finally
left. Just on the edge of town, the driver stopped to buy gas. I could
not believe that in all the time we had been waiting they had not
even bothered to fill up. I could only guess that the earlier com-
ings and goings were part of some bargaining process to get the
best gas price possible. I watched the driver work between three
different salesmen. He drank a cup of coffee while the carboys
watched, then he made his decision with great ceremony.

The victorious seller hopped on the runner board and we circled back the other side of town where our driver tested the supply, smelling it and holding a sample up to the light as if it were a
fine wine.

"Perfect!" I felt like yelling, "Let's get on with it!" But I remembered what had happened to Mungo Park.

The sun had just set when we pulled out again. There was tarmac for a short way through the desert, and then the road broke
up and there was only desert and the sky glowing orange on one
side and midnight blue on the other. The air was cool on my face
for the first time all day, and even with the rumbling of the truck
I could feel the silence all around. None of the other passengers
were speaking, but I could sense their excitement. They were a
pretty motley bunch, with yellow teeth, ragged turbans, and dirty
clothes. I imagined that they were all running away from trouble
or heading off to find work. Wherever they were going, everyone
seemed pleased to be moving, especially the carboys who leaned
out of the cab and hung on the side and back of the truck, yelling
to each other and joking around.

After about an hour and a half, we had our first breakdown.

"Bad gas," one of the carboys confided to me after a great deal
of banging under the truck. The fuel line was cleaned and then
later, when it broke down again, all the gas in the tank was
drained and filtered. Then we got stuck in the sand in the middle
of the night. It was the first of many times that the carboys had to
swing into action, digging us out and laying the sand ladders in
front of the wheels. Sometimes when the truck got moving, they
would keep picking up the ladders and running to the front,
throwing them down again under the wheels to keep us going.
Later, when it got even sandier, there were times when they would
end up running along behind the truck, trying in vain to catch us,
the big sand ladders held above their heads. The driver didn't dare
slow down on the soft sand and wouldn't stop for them to catch
up until we hit solid ground again. Of course, then we would sit

and wait for them to show up huffing and puffing, sometimes half an hour later. The driver would lean against the truck and smoke a cigarette and then tease them when they arrived. I watched very little of this the first night because I was so exhausted, but later it became practically a spectator sport, or perhaps a minor opera, complete with yelling and hurt feelings and dramatic posturing on the part of the participants.

The burlap date sacks provided a surprisingly comfortable seat and a good view. After a while, everyone had staked out a place. I was right on top in the middle, nestled in a spot that was cozy to lie down and sleep on at night and comfortable for sitting up during the day. From there, I could see in every direction, and the scenery was quietly breathtaking. The river was almost always in sight, and the further north we went, the closer the yellow Saharan sands would come to the river's edge. Sometimes there were fishing villages, but mostly it was just low arid hills and wide open space. Occasionally we would stop for a bathroom break and everyone would scatter into the small dunes. But most of the time we just drove day and night with occasional stops for the driver to sleep a short time in the wee hours of the morning.

At first the other passengers watched everything I did, curious about my gear and strange habits. They loved my convertible khakis and would comment back and forth to each other in Bambara as I went through the ritual of zipping off the legs in the morning and then zipping them back on again as it cooled down at night. One of them who spoke French would translate for the others, asking me questions and then relaying my answers. They couldn't seem to imagine why I was reading and writing all the time, and I couldn't imagine what they might be thinking about all day as they watched the scenery slowly roll by. It wasn't long before everyone had run out of food and we had all started eating dates to get by. At first I was just occasionally sneaking a few through a little hole in the bag under me, but soon we were all eating them openly, one after another after another. They seemed stale to me — brittle and chewy at the same time. But every time I got thoroughly sick of them and swore them off, I would be so hungry a few hours later that I would eat another handful.

As we got closer to Timbuktu we drove right along the river and there were more little towns. Small sand dunes were on one side and the blue Niger River on the other, but still no clear road. Everyone was so tired and hungry by the third day that we began stopping for a couple of hours at a time to cook meals. The carboys would gather up some reeds and twigs for a fire, and the driver would spend an hour and a half cooking rice with some fish or meat in it. I was still wary of eating meat, but when I smelled it cooking, I just couldn't resist. The meals were divided into two bowls for everyone to eat out of with their hands, which seemed a little too intimate for me. I would sit in the circle with the others, but I insisted on taking my portion in a tin cooking pot and then eating with my utensils. They thought this was very funny. I figured that if I couldn't inspect every bit of food I ate, I could at least try to minimize the germs.

After a while, it began to feel like we were a team and the others became less preoccupied by my novelty. As I got to know them, it was clear that I had been mistaken about them being a rough crowd. The other passengers were all relatively well-off, I found out. They were merchants, students, and teachers. They had all paid the same fare as I had, which was not something that the average West African could afford. The young man who drove the truck owned it and another one with his father, and they had very high status in their community. The carboys also were considered to have very good positions. I watched them with interest as they banged on a flat tire in the midday sun, sweating and smiling as they worked, while the driver in his greasy black-and-yellow baseball shirt smoked a cigarette and stared out at the nearby desert.

In the middle of the fourth night, one of the carboys woke me up and told me that we were near Timbuktu. A little while later I climbed down from the truck in the dark with two other passengers and said good-bye to the rest of the gang who were continuing on to other towns. Even the driver, who had begun speaking to me and joking around with me a little towards the end, seemed sad to see me go. "Timbuktu, five kilometers," he said a couple of times, pointing north so that I would know where to go.

He pulled away into the darkness, and I stood alone in the cold desert as the other two passengers walked off in separate directions. I didn't feel like hiking in the dark and I was tired from days of broken sleep, so I pitched my tent behind a small rise and hoped no one would run over me. I didn't wake up until nearly eight the next morning, when I heard little scuffing noises outside my tent. I unzipped the cover and two small boys were staring at me, smiling.

"Bonjour," I said, and their eyes got wide. When I said a couple of things in English they giggled. Each had a "Paris-Dakar Rally" T-shirt from the previous year's race, and a little toy car made from scrap wires and discarded cans that someone had cut up for them. There wasn't a building in sight and I couldn't imagine where they had come from. But they looked pretty healthy, so I didn't worry about their well-being. When I asked them where Timbuktu was, they pointed in different directions. I gave them each a few dates and they played with my compass and my harmonica while I packed up the tent. They followed me for a little while as I headed in the direction I thought the city was, but eventually they got distracted by something one of them found in the sand and they trailed off. As I walked along, I realized that they had never actually said anything and had never stopped smiling — the official silent greeting committee of Timbuktu.

A LONG WAY FROM HOME

TIMBUKTU WAS NOT WHAT I had expected. The walk was a long five kilometers, but I found the main road and buildings gradually began to appear along it. First there was a series of relatively new buildings that appeared to have sprung up haphazardly on either side of the road — not exactly the intriguing ancient architecture I had been expecting. These modern buildings ended at the gates of the old city, a clump of streets and old buildings surrounded by the desert. As I approached the main gate, a pack of teenage boys practically knocked me over trying to offer their services as guides. They were almost as pushy as kids I had met in Morocco, but when I agreed to hire one of them for a dollar for half a day, they all calmed down and sat back to wait for the next tourist to come along. At that time of year, at least, the prospects weren't numerous.

My guide's name was Asou and he was very nice, but I soon
realized I had heard most of his French in the first minute of our
acquaintance. He said that he could take me to a very good hotel
and then walked me through the city to a brand new French chain
hotel sitting in the dunes a few hundred yards west of town. It was
a Sofitel — a sort of French Hyatt, with rooms for seventy-five
dollars a night. I was so surprised to find such a place in Timbuktu
that I nearly pulled out my credit card and took a room.

I decided instead to just get some breakfast on the terrace. The
staff turned up their noses at my appearance, but there did not seem
to be any other customers and it was so nice to have a good meal
that I didn't care. I tried to get Asou to sit with me, but he refused.
Instead he went off to see if he could find my friend Dave. The
name did not seem familiar to him, but "Corps de la Paix" brought
some recognition. When he came back, he had found someone, but
he could not take me there until noon, he said. When I tried to get
more information, he would only say, "After, after."

So after paying six dollars for a coffee and some wonderfully
good croissants, we set off to explore what was left of the great
city. There was a set route he wanted to take me on, mostly to
show me all the best doors in town. The two lasting vestiges
of ancient Timbuktu are the roadside bread ovens and the ornate
wooden doors. When Gordon Laing finally became the first
European to set foot in the city in 1826 after spending a horrify-
ing year in the Sahara, he had found that instead of being a
gilded city, Timbuktu was a rough trading outpost, the local merchants living in fear of the Tuareg nomads who came riding out
of the desert on their camels every few months to collect tribute.
In the hope of avoiding notice, the locals tried to make the outside of their homes look very poor, and they imported heavy
wood from as far away as Greece to build doors that would keep
the Tuaregs out. It was a cat-and-mouse game that worked fairly
well until the French moved in from Senegal to occupy the town
in 1893.

Now the Sahara Desert has advanced around the city. Most of the people have left, except a few hundred who are supported by tourism and the help of aid groups like Africare, Oxfam, and the Peace Corps. The streets are still lined with windowless walls and the locals have kept the unique, sturdily decorated doors intact. I was touched by the rugged beauty of these classical doors, with their dark wood and tarnished silver fittings, but I kept getting distracted by the sand drifts in the streets and the way the Sahara seemed to be looming in the background. It was as if the whole place would soon be swallowed by the dunes. Indeed, if it were not for the tourist interest, Timbuktu probably would have been abandoned to the sands long ago.

The official tour ended at a Tuareg tent in the sands just outside the north walls. I would not have gone in, but I needed a knife and I knew that knives were an important part of the Tuareg culture. After a traditional tea ceremony in which mint tea was mixed back and forth between steaming pots, I was shown a whole array of beautiful jewelry and knives. The Tuareg man was not entirely comfortable with his position as a salesman. He seemed very proud and averse to showing any kind of deference toward me, even when he was making the tea. I couldn't imagine him staying in that shop for more than six months at a time. Perhaps after a good run of sales, I thought, he would go travel the desert for a few years and come back to Timbuktu only to exact tribute from the manager at the Sofitel. I paid ten dollars for a small Tuareg knife with designs etched in the blade and on the leather case. I wanted to buy more to help spring him sooner, but the knife was all I needed, and I didn't want to be frivolous.

Afterward, we went to the marketplace in the center of town where a few vendors were selling some fruit, canned food, and souvenirs from small piles. They acted like they thought I was going to spend a thousand dollars, pushing fruit and cans and trinkets at me. I bought some more canned milk and canned meat and sardines, along with some expensive tangerines. Flies were everywhere and skinny dogs sniffed their way around the square. I couldn't believe that this was Timbuktu. It was so dilapidated and one-dimensional compared to what I had been expecting. Its past didn't resonate at all. Instead, I was confronted by a sense of its bleak future. If I hadn't had Asou to help me deal with the people, I probably would have fled to the Sofitel.

At least it will be fun to see Dave, I thought, as I tried to keep the flies out of my ears. At noon all the vendors started closing up shop and Asou and I went to find the Peace Corps office down the main road where I had come in. Although I had never received replies to my letters from Paris and Niger, I had just assumed that Dave would be there, expecting my arrival. But instead I was taken to a surly British Oxfam worker who said that no one from the Peace Corps had been there for a couple of years. He was pretty sure he had heard of Dave and thought he was stationed in Mopti, the next big town upriver, about 250 miles southwest.

I felt like someone had punched me in the stomach. I couldn't believe it. Since I had crossed into Niger a few weeks earlier, I had been feeling a need to rest and regroup a bit, something I had pur- posely put off until I found Dave. I couldn't believe that I was going to have to keep moving. I felt instantly depressed. Timbuktu had taken on such strong symbolic connotations in my mind. It was the spark that had set my plan in motion and it was supposed to be a symbol of remote adventure and self-reliance. But I sure didn't want to stay in Timbuktu for a few days by myself.

I picked up my bag at the Sofitel, paid Asou a good tip, and then set out to walk six miles out to the river at Kabara. A taxi driver followed me out of the town and tried to get fifteen dollars to take me.

"Maybe in New York," I told him.

It took a couple of hours to make the hike. As I walked along, with all the food and water I had gotten for three days on the river, my pack felt heavier and heavier. I couldn't believe that Timbuktu was such a disappointment. I had been pushing so hard to get there that it seemed ridiculous to just move on the same day, but I had to put my mind on the next destination and keep moving. At least, I thought, the travel further upriver would be easier. Everyone had told me that there would be no problem getting from Timbuktu to Mopti because there were "many" boats. My guidebook had shown a picture of a big, double-decker paddle steamer that looked like something right off the Mississippi. It said that two or three of these boats ran regularly between Mopti and Kabara and that smaller bargelike boats called "pinasses" left a few times a day. I had originally been planning to take the big boat and just sit back with my feet up on the rail, drinking beer with other travelers. But the Oxfam guy had shot that idea down as well, saying that with the water so low, the pinasse was the only way to go.

When I got to Kabara, I could see one of the paddle boats listing in the mud a few hundred yards from the shore. An old man told me that maybe by March the river would get high enough to float it again. When I asked him about the pinasses, he said there were none now and that I should try the dock at Kourema, a few miles upriver. He said there would be many there. A crowd had gathered around us while we talked and when I set out on the path to Kourema, half of them followed me for nearly a mile, just out of curiosity. As I walked along, I cursed the delays and I cursed the people gawking at me. I still was not adjusted to Africa. The lack of infrastructure and the abundance of leisure time was maddening because I was always so intent on my destination — moving, moving. Everyone kept telling me "pas de problème" and "Il y a beaucoup," but it seemed like there were always "problems" and there were never "many" of anything except flies and gawkers. Even the path along the river to the next village did not make sense. Twice the path came to a dead end at the water's edge and I had to backtrack and take meandering routes that seemed to mock me with pointless turns as I sweated under the weight of my pack.

I got as close to the town as I could before dark and ended up setting camp about a mile and a half away. In the morning I went back to sleep for about fifteen minutes after the alarm on my watch beeped, and then packed up as quickly as I could because it was getting light fast. As I headed down the road toward the dock, I could see one of the long, black, wooden pinasses pulling away. My heart started racing and I picked up my pace. By the time I got there five minutes later, the boat was already getting small as it moved up river. "Don't worry, there'll be others," I kept telling myself, but looking around I realized that there were only a few of the small pirogues. A couple of rough-looking fishermen with motorized pirogues offered to chase the boat for twenty dollars, but I declined, sure that some others would be coming. When I finally found someone who spoke French, they told me that there would not be another boat for three days. By that time the pinasse was too far away to catch.

I was so frustrated and angry that I snapped at a group of locals who had been following me as I ran back and forth trying to figure the situation out. They thought this was wonderful. They hadn't seen anyone so entertaining in a long while. I tried to calm down and find some other options, but the little town was dead and there was no choice for me but to go back to Timbuktu. By the time I left, there was practically a cheering throng to send me on my way.

As I was walking down the road an hour later, mad at the world, a French UNICEF worker came along and gave me a ride in her jeep. She cringed when I spoke her language, but we were able to make just enough small talk during the drive to keep me from acting on an impulsive desire to hijack her jeep and take off with it. I even had the more disturbing thought that it would be wonderful if Henri would show up with one of the Renaults so that I could go driving around with him some more. "My kingdom for a jeep!" I felt like screaming out the window.

In Timbuktu the people seemed even more persistent and annoying than the day before, and Asou was nowhere to be found.

After asking all around, I found out that I could catch a ride with a mail truck heading upriver if I got there early enough in the morning. To get a shower and some peace, I took a room in a rough, state-run hotel near the market square. I stayed in the desert shower nearly an hour, washing all of my clothes before I got out. I then spent three dollars on a warm beer that I nursed all evening while reading my guide and trying to plan out a route from Bamako to Bangui in the Central African Republic. "Having problems is one thing," I wrote later that night in my journal, "but having them be a public spectacle is another."

I also noted that the Africans seemed to have a peculiar and useful habit of laughing at my aggressive behavior. "If I learn anything in Africa," I wrote, "it will be patience and tenacity."

During the night the mosquitoes and mice were so bad that I finally had to set up my tent out in the courtyard. In the morning I jumped out of my sleeping bag at four o'clock and was at the post office by four-thirty. I found the mail truck and got a seat to Niafounke, 110 miles southeast, where the driver said he was sure that I could find a boat. He gave me one of the two front seats in the brand new Toyota Land Cruiser, while fourteen people squeezed into the back. I felt both guilty and thankful every time I turned around. There were almost as many people as pieces of mail, and I guessed that at least half the mail in his small bag was mine, including seven letters and thirteen postcards that I had written on the date truck and mailed the day before. I had been thinking that I couldn't get much farther from home than Timbuktu.

QUIET TIME

AFTER A BUMPY, SIX-HOUR RIDE through rutted tracks and deep sand that would have taken a week for the date truck to get through, we arrived in Niafounke. When the mail truck let me off in the center of town, I hurried straight down to the river, sure that a boat would be leaving any second. There were none there and none in sight in either direction on the wide river. I hurried back to a little store and bought some rice and a couple of orange Fantas, and then rushed back to the beach. I asked around about boats and was told that one would be leaving for Mopti that evening, "ce soir." I was relieved and glad that I hadn't paid to ride two more days in the mail truck to Mopti, because I really did want to travel on the river.

But when I was still on the beach the next morning, shivering in my sleeping bag with my tent still packed, just in case a boat came, I was not as sure. I was then told that the boat would come at "midi," and then "après midi," and then towards the end of the day again, "ce soir." Soon I knew that they had no idea when the next pinasse would come, only that one was expected — probably the one I had missed in Kourema a few days before. Every once in a while a fishing boat would come in, or a smaller boat carrying a family, and when I asked some of them about rides, they all said the same thing — just wait, a boat would be coming. For them and for me, it seemed, there was always one just beyond on the horizon.

And so I waited. I cooked some food, started reading a new book, wrote some letters and thought about home. The book I was reading was, *A Documentary History of the United States*, which I had picked up in Paris. It used emblematic documents from each decade to tell the intellectual history of the country, and though it had sat untouched in my pack for two-and-a-half months, now I was thrilled to have it. I felt starved for Americana. The pure rationality of Thomas Paine's *Common Sense*, and Jefferson's *Declaration of Independence* seemed brilliant and awe-inspiring when read in the political context of West Africa. After seeing how the police operated, how neglected the infrastructure was, and hearing stories about how the leaders of Niger and Mali and many of the other countries enriched themselves by stealing aid money and raiding their own treasuries, I began to change my mind about the state of politics in America. For the first time since I had interned for a senator, I found myself feeling grateful and fortunate for the order and rationality of the American government. It seemed impossible to me that some countries founded two hundred years after the United States could have thoroughly rejected our ideals of individual dignity, natural rights, and government for the common good.

Talking to the local children, though, I felt there was reason to believe that things might begin to change in the future. By the second day, I had picked up a regular gang of kids who came before and after school, and even during their lunch breaks, to see if

I was still there. Some of the smaller children were afraid of me at first and I took to roaring at them and laughing with the others when they ran away. They showed me some of their notebooks from school — all very neat and filled with surprisingly advanced mathematics, French, geography, and cultural studies. I set up my tent for the second night and played soccer with the kids as the sun was setting. When it started to get late, they filtered away, but in the morning they were back again.

From my spot on the beach, I could see many activities of the town. Early in the morning, just as it was getting light, people came to bathe. Men stripped down before sitting in the water with their legs straight out, floating downriver a little and splashing as they went. The women wore thin, muslin coverings which could be art-fully shifted around, to allow for the bathing of one exposed part at a time. Each night and each morning the women also came down to the river to wash their pots and pans, or to get water for their gardens. They would talk with each other as they worked, and no one seemed to mind me being there. Sometimes they would even smile as they shuffled by with heavy containers balanced on their heads. One day I saw a rooster making his rounds amongst the hens, and an old man whipping a crowd of children who had been making too much noise for his liking. Another day a man rode by on an elaborately decorated horse and a small boy walked back and forth with a dead snake. In the evening a skinny bull wandered up to a nearby house, bellowed, and walked right in.

On the third night, under a full moon, I watched a small pinasse come in loaded with firewood and a very tired crew. The men jumped into the water before they were aground and families came running down to greet them. Kids jumped and yelled, the whole scene beautifully silhouetted against the silvery river. I crawled out of my tent and checked to see if they were going further, but they were not. They were home, they said, at least for a while.

In the Sahel, I began to see, it doesn't take very long before the quiet spirit of the region begins to work on any visitor, drawing you in, giving you hints and glimpses of its beauty, changing you slowly. After a few days, I realized that the pace of the river was working on me. Though things didn't work at my preferred pace, I began to see that they had a beautifully simple and quiet pacing of their own. My anger over the delays disappeared and I felt lucky to be a passive observer in that place. It felt like the river was moving the world and it was clear that the local people had priority. I would be served when my turn came, or perhaps when I quieted down enough to be able to see their logic and move at their pace. For them, there was almost never a destination, just a path of moments. One moment fully absorbed, and the next and the next. Sitting there on the beach for so long, I realized that I had been in Africa for nearly a month before allowing myself to be touched by anything African.

Late in the afternoon of my fourth day on the beach, two large, canopied pinasses came around the bend downriver and floated up sideways along the beach. There was much excitement at their arrival, followed by a flurry of trading and people coming and going between the town and the beach. They took me on board the second boat and said that it would be "three to ten days" to Mopti.

Each boat was about sixty feet long and ten feet wide, with a weathered green canopy covering it from bow to stern, open all along the sides. Where each of the canopy poles were placed, there were low cross beams inside the boat, and these divided the boat into eight sections. The captain, his crew, and their families were traveling and living in the back half of the boat, while the passengers rode in the front sections. In the middle there was an open kitchen, and much to my amazement as I got on board, the women were busily cooking over a small fire. Every section besides the kitchen was loaded right up to the gunwales with cargo, so the fire and the women cooking were down lower than everything else and it was possible for them to stand up while they worked.

I was given a spot in the first section in front of the kitchen. It seemed to be the bachelor's quarters. There were already five younger African men there when I arrived and they politely moved enough to give me room for my pack and my legs. Like the date truck, everyone was sitting on bags full of produce — this time rice and corn that wasn't nearly as comfortable as dates because it packed down too hard. Under that, I found out later, there were boxes full of corn oil and vegetable oil, and then finally, big slabs of salt that looked like slate or dirty styrofoam. In the sections in front of the bachelor's pad, there were two families and then a few older couples.

When I boarded, everyone was watching me. I said "hello" a few times and smiled and nodded, but only those nearby smiled back. The rest just stared, wide-eyed. Soon we were floating up the river directly into the fading sunset. I was glad when it finally got dark so they couldn't all watch me anymore. The boat chugged upriver at a turtle's pace, the engine working rhythmically in the stern while the women hummed in the kitchen. Up ahead the other boat — an identical twin — worked its way through the channels of the shallow river. Little pirogues moved past us going the other way, the men working their poles and paddles in long strokes. On the banks, small fires glowed orange and red next to grass huts.

Until the moon came up, all was darkness except the touch of firelight playing on the canopy above the kitchen. And all was quiet except the soft engine, the women's humming, and the waves against the bow. I could smell the food cooking, oily smoke wafting up from the kitchen, and it made me very hungry. I was sad that I had not brought more food with me — all I had left were my sardines and canned meat and a little bit of rice. I knew I would be hungry every time they cooked and I resigned myself to sparse eating on the way to Mopti and then some big eating with

Dave once I got there. But soon a large bowl of rice and fish was passed to each section and I was asked to join with the others. I didn't even have time to get out my bowl and separate out my portion. I used my spoon while the others used their hands, making myself eat slowly because it was so delicious and I wasn't sure there was enough for everybody.

When the others got out their blankets and pulled their hoods over their heads, I slid into my sleeping bag and reclined as best I could in the confined space, thinking for a long time before I fell asleep how extraordinary it was to be in this strange and wonderful place.

In the morning I woke to the sounds of the women cooking again. It was cold, but a hot bowl of rice porridge arrived before I was out of my bag long enough to get chilly. The bachelors all gathered around the bowl and slurped loudly while they ate, clearly pleased that I liked the food as well. As the sun rose, the temperature rose too and it was not long before I was wearing only a T-shirt, shorts, and sandals, perspiring in the stifling air. The others huddled in long layers of clothing. For them it was the middle of winter. Every time I looked up, at least half a dozen people were watching me and I had to move subtly whenever I took anything out of my pack or everyone in the boat would focus on what I was doing. I was an endless curiosity for all of them, especially the kids who were a couple of sections up. I would constantly hear people talking about the "toubab," in their conversations. This must be how it feels to be a movie star or a member of the royal family, I thought, having every move scrutinized and discussed, even in your presence.

But the bachelors, at least, seemed to get used to me pretty quickly. One of them, who spoke a bit of French and served as the official translator for the others, seemed intensely pleased to have me on board. He would explain each new dish to me and watch with delight as I took my first bite. He would question me about my equipment and my travels and what I was reading and writing. And all day long, as he tuned his radio back and forth between stations, trying to find music clear enough to listen to, he would stop on any non-African song he found to see if it was one of my favorites.

"C'est bon, non?" he would ask with a big smile as Jimmy Hendrix or some Eurofunk tune scratched its way out of the speakers.

"Excellent," I'd say, and they would all smile and we'd groove together until the station faded or until I pleaded with him to change it to some "musique africain."

Every few hours we would pull up to the shore and slide a long plank down to the sand so that we could walk to shore without getting wet. Usually this would be at a small village and some of the cargo would be unloaded. We'd have time to run a little ways from the river and go to the bathroom. At first I was pretty worried about bathroom breaks, but the captain wasn't only paying attention to the depth of the channels, and we always seemed to stop just in time.

When the gangplank was up across the gunwales, it acted as a temporary shelf for the kitchen and it stuck out about four feet on each side of the boat, like small wings. As we went along, I took to sitting out on the wings in the middle of the day to catch the breezes while I read or wrote. When it got too hot, I would dip my cooking pot into the muddy river and splash a little on myself. Soon, I was pouring the whole thing over my head. This always caused a big stir within the boat, but after so many weeks in the desert, the water felt so wonderful I couldn't resist.

When I got tired of being scrutinized, I would climb up on the roof with my binoculars and watch from there as the scenery slowly changed. On one of these rooftop excursions, I fell asleep and my binoculars went clattering down the roof into the water. I woke up, jumped quickly down while keeping an eye on them, and then ran along the gunwales trying to reach them before we went by. But I couldn't get to them fast enough. Impulsively I dove into the river after them. Everyone woke up from their afternoon naps in a hurry and clamored to the side. The captain roared with laughter and then circled around to get me. I had discovered that my binoculars not only floated, but were waterproof, and fortunately I didn't bump into any hippos or snakes in the murky water.

As we went further south, dry, brown grass appeared along the banks. Then the long grass got greener and thicker and trees began appearing. We passed more and more traffic — pirogues poling their way upriver, medium-sized transport boats chugging along with whole families camped in grass huts on the back deck, fishing boats running nets out from the shore. There were grass hut villages with cows and goats that would have to be moved miles away when the river came back up. And occasionally there were a few hippos yawning out in the middle of the current or wrestling in the shallows like sumos, and then diving for minutes at a time as we passed.

Every once in a while one of the motors would break down or we would get stuck on a sandbar. The captain's son would jump off the bow and start pushing, or dive into the engine box and come out a bit later greasy and proud. I had thought at first that I would be able to get wellwater or the ubiquitous Fantas in the villages along the way, but at our pace it was impossible to wait for villages, and I began drinking the muddy water out of the river like the others. At first I would filter it three times through my white T-shirt and then boil it and add iodine tablets. It would still be muddy looking, but I just drank a little at a time. When I didn't get sick, I became more daring and eventually I would skip the boiling so that I wouldn't use up all my cooking gas, just filtering it once and adding the iodine tablets. It wasn't long before my white T-shirt was almost orange.

On the third day we stopped at a small beach and unloaded a good portion of our cargo. I had suspected that we were carrying aid food from what I had seen come off earlier, but now I could clearly see the labels on the bags and boxes. All of the rice and corn that we had been sitting on had a U.S. shield printed on the bottom with two hands shaking and the words "Donated by the People of the United States of America." Fifty-five of these bags were unloaded along with twenty boxes of U.S. vegetable oil with six gallons in each, thirty boxes of canned mackerel donated by Japan (my loathsome sardines), and forty boxes of the Danish canned meat that I had been buying along the way.

When I asked, the captain told me that it was all for free distribution, but he seemed nervous about my interest and would not allow me to take any photos. Of course, I knew that some of the aid food was sold (I had been buying it myself in the markets) but I couldn't help but wonder at what point the trading and selling began. Was it sold from the top down, as soon as it arrived in the country? Or did the locals merely trade unwanted stuff away once they had received their portions?

From then on, we had to ride on top of the salt slabs which were dirty and bug-ridden and stacked on their narrow sides rather than flat down, making it impossible to sleep on them or sit in one position for any length of time. They seemed more like big, flat rocks than any salt I'd ever seen, and I was told that they had come from the Saharan salt mines way in the north, where the most dangerous and the most political of the prisoners were sent to die — the desert Siberia of Mali. If it was so awful just sitting on the dirty slabs, I couldn't even imagine what the conditions in the mines could be like.

Fortunately it wasn't too much farther to Mopti, and on the last night we slept on the shore because the channels were too shallow to navigate at night. I slept restlessly in my tent, worried in my dreams that the boat would somehow leave without me. Near midnight I awoke completely startled to see three turbaned Tuaregs casually surveying our camp. "Toubab, asalamo alaïkoum," one of them said loudly, though I had tried to pretend I was asleep. It meant, "Whiteboy, peace be with you." They walked around the campsite a bit and then drifted off into the darkness.

A LITTLE SIGHTSEEING

WHEN WE FINALLY GOT TO MOPTI I headed straight to the Peace Corps hostel and asked for Dave. The volunteers who were there seemed annoyed to be interrupted in the middle of what sounded like a major gripe session. Dave had not been there in two years, they told me. He was now working as a trainer in the capital at Bamako. I felt so deflated that I ignored their disdainful stares and practically insisted that they let me shower and sleep at their hostel. They begrudgingly offered me a bed, though they said they were "tired of tourists crashing here and drinking all the beer." I made sure that I bought my own beer and felt a little less offended when two Peace Corps volunteers on leave from Liberia showed up and were treated with the same hospitality.

The newcomers, Steve and Darrell, wrote their reception off to the generally poor morale in the Mali Peace Corps, but they said that things were worse in Liberia and any change of scenery was good. We hit it off right away and for a few days I reveled in speaking English and running around with them. We ate dinner at a Chinese restaurant in the town and drank beer in a riverside café. I asked them about the aid food I had seen and Steve just shrugged and said, "It's corrupt from the top down. But maybe it creates a local trade in goods that wouldn't be there otherwise — and that's aid of some sort."

"Unless, of course, it suppresses local production, which it well might," Darrell replied. They tried not to be cynical, but sometimes they couldn't help it, they said.

And after I got to know them a little better, Steve added, "At the very best we are not hurting them. I worry all the time that most of what we do is beneficial only to us."

Using my guidebook and some inside information from their Peace Corps friends, we took a bush-taxi — a white Toyota pickup loaded with more than twenty people in back — out to the Dogon Country and then rented mopeds to get to the escarpment where the Dogon people still live. We were each given a grass-covered hut for a couple of nights at a Dogon home, and saw some of the art and anthropomorphic architecture that have made the region famous.

The Dogons have an ancient belief system which shapes their approach to life that is as intricate and complex as any on earth. For them, everything functions as a balance of opposites and every activity is ordered according to beliefs and symbols embedded in their collective mythology. Their fields are laid out in spirals of alternating crops and their homes and villages mirror the shape of the human body, with corresponding positions holding symbolic importance. Much of what I had always considered primitive African art and culture, I found out, actually came from this one small area. And while tourist-driven commercialism swirled on the periphery of their existence — from the moped rentals to the salesmen pushing "newly unburied" art objects — the Dogons seemed to have remained mostly a quiet, contemplative people, farming and trying to stay to themselves. Often they retreated to the ceremonial caves built into the cliffs above or below their villages. They were almost gnomelike in appearance, short with pointy hats and round, jolly faces. They walked around with axes and hoes over their shoulders and were quick to say hello, and quick to run shyly away.

When the Dogons were first "discovered" in the early 1900s, anthropologists were intrigued by their expansive knowledge of the heavens. Though they had no telescopes or other scientific equipment, they believed in a heliocentric solar system. They spoke of Jupiter's moons and Saturn's rings, and they held the birght star, Sirius B, as the center of their mythology. A team of European astronomers was dispatched to find out how they knew so much about the solar system. In different villages, the scientists were told by the local people that the Dogons had gotten their knowledge of the heavens from the occupants of a spaceship that had visited them long ago. They also spoke about the "eleven planets" in our solar system and because of this obvious, simple error, the scientists finally dismissed their astronomical knowledge as arbitrary. The Dogon's planetary ideas were not given serious consideration again until just after my visit, when high-powered telescopes and advanced orbital calculations revealed the possible existence of two "previously unknown" planets, bringing the total to the eleven that the Dogans had always believed existed.

When we had finished touring the escarpment, we checked out some of the gift shops in Bandiagara where we had rented the mopeds. There were close to a dozen of them filled with "ancient artifacts" that were actually recent carvings that had been chipped and rolled in ashes to make them look older. The best of them had been buried for a while, sometimes five or six years Darrell found out while speaking Bambara with some of the locals on the street. As we looked for a place to eat dinner that night, we saw a great rush of locals heading to the community hall. It seemed like the whole village had come out for the evening. We followed them to see what was going on, hoping to see an interesting ceremony or at least a political event. Instead, a Betamax version of *Rambo* was playing on an old nineteen-inch TV.

We left as soon as we could in the morning. When we got back to Mopti I said good-bye to Darrell and Steve who were heading north into the desert. I then hopped in another bush-taxi to go to Djenne, fifty miles to the southwest. The trip took six hours, but the driver let me sit in the front, this time with two other passengers.

My guidebook had a picture of the Djenne "mud mosque" on the cover, so it was naturally on my list of "must see" sites. It is a terra-cotta mosque made from straw and sand and dirt, and every year the local people rebuild it after the heavy rains wash away the mud. The lighter rains during the rest of the year round the edges and sculpt the towers like Popsicles. It looked more like a sand-castle than any building I had ever seen, and it was strangely beautiful to look at from the outside. But inside it was dark and claustrophobic. The local Muslim men were going through their prayers while the women and tourists stayed behind a partition at the far end of the building. I felt disappointed because it didn't match my expectations, but for a long time afterward, I kept re-membering the way the shadows of the men bowing and standing in prayer worked between the columns, the way the dust from the sand floor hung in the thin shafts of light, the way the women shuffled restlessly behind their screen.

Outside, I waded into the big market, the other reason that most of the locals came to Djenne. It was just the opposite of the mosque — color and noise and action everywhere. I was far enough south that there was local produce and plenty of other things for sale. I saw fruits and vegetables that I had forgotten about, and some that I had never seen before. I bought peanuts, tomatoes, avocados, hot peppers, and rice. That night I mixed them together in a super hot batch of "flamaya," my favorite traveling concoction, to celebrate the beginning of my fourth month on the road.

In the local tourist hostel, I shared a room with a guy from Washington, D.C., who kept mentioning that he had gone to Harvard Law School and that he had once served in the Peace Corps. We spent the evening drinking on the porch with an Italian friend, and a seasoned British aid worker who told fascinating stories about the "guerrilla" relief work he had done with Oxfam in Chad during the civil war there. The nomadic tribes were too proud to take food handouts, he said, but their normal trading partners had been wiped out by the war. Oxfam tried everything they could think of to give them aid, and finally they had to use high aerial photography to plot the peoples' movements in the desert. Then they would drop the food in their path. If the nomads came upon the boxes, they would take the food. If they missed it, Oxfam would just try again a few weeks later. He had no idea, he said, if any of these nomads had survived the war. The Harvard lawyer tried to compete with his own war stories from his Peace Corps days and his work on Capitol Hill. But the rest of us barely listened, staring out at the stars over the sandy hills nearby, listening to the noises of the night and the sounds of prayer echoing again from the mud mosque.

It took two days to find a ride south of Djenne and when I left, the Italian and the Harvard lawyer went with me. We piled into the back of a medium-sized transport truck with thirty other people and a couple tons of grain stacked on the roof. The seats were hard benches arranged in rows like church pews. Diesel exhaust poured in through the open back. About every half hour the truck would break down, and not long into the trip small white maggots started dropping from the ceiling, having squeezed their way out of the grain sacks. The truck had to go all the way back to Mopti before heading to Bamako, and after nine hours in a carbon-monoxide haze, we were very discouraged to find ourselves just passing the signs for Djenne again. The Harvard lawyer added to the discomfort by droning on and on about "the insanity of Africa."

"If they would carry a reasonable load, these trucks could go twice as fast and break down half as often," he said, "That would give them three times as many trips without all the troubles, but if you try to tell them, they just shrug. It's insane. Every time I go away I forget, but this is it . . ."

The Italian got sick twice when we stopped. I sat with a T-shirt doubled up over my face, trying to meditate on a plan for getting all the way to Kenya after Bamako. Darrell and Steve had been singing the praises of Central and East Africa and had suggested taking an Air Afrique flight to Bangui, the capital of the Central African Republic (C.A.R.), rather than traveling overland along the southern coast. I was worried about the time required to go overland and the money required to fly, but the big question was whether or not I wanted to see Togo, Ghana, the Ivory Coast, and some of the other countries that dot the coastline of the Gulf of Guinea south of Mali. As we limped along in the crowded, rickety old truck, plagued by maggots, I was starting to feel that I had just about gotten my fill of traveling in West Africa.

In the middle of the night, we stopped at a makeshift truck stop that had hole-in-the-ground outhouses and a couple of tea stands. The other passengers piled out of the truck and the driver went to see about getting a new tire. I sat down at one of the stands and ordered a coffee with milk. There was a young man behind the plank bar and I watched him put two small pieces of wood on the fire and stoke it carefully. He poured four ladles of water from a wooden barrel into an iron tea pot and placed it above the fire. On the ground in the corner was a straw mattress and a single blanket. The man looked sleepy but he smiled as he worked.

I could hear crickets and the hiss of the fire, and the sounds of people sleeping nearby. I watched him measure the syrupy condensed milk into each mug and then filter the coffee and pour the mixture back and forth to get everything well mixed and hot. He brought out some greasy beignets, and had a cup of coffee with me and the others who had come over. I had been feeling irritated — stuck there in the middle of the night and stuck heading further west when I needed to go east to get to Kenya. But the warm drink and the African doughnuts tasted so good that I settled down and soon found myself hoping that the truck wouldn't get fixed too quickly so that we could just stay for a while in that peaceful place.

PRIORITIES

WHEN WE GOT NEAR BAMAKO, late the next morning, the truck spent the last forty-five minutes driving out of the way on dirt roads and through back neighborhoods so that we wouldn't encounter any police inspections. When we finally climbed out of the truck downtown, maggots spilled out onto the road and we were so frazzled from the ride that we barely said our good-byes before heading shakily down the tree-lined streets.

When I found the Peace Corps office it was bustling with activity because thirty new volunteers had just flown in. They looked amazingly fresh, their clothes all clean and their eyes darting about. I wondered how they felt flying straight from Washington into this radically different world which was going to be their home for two years. Just wait till they see the toilets, I thought.

My friend Dave was out at the training site getting things ready for the new recruits, but he had gotten word from the people in Mopti that I was coming and he had set things up for me to stay in an empty room at the trainers' house where he lived. I was so relieved. I had longed for clean beds and clean bathrooms, and I was not disappointed. I wanted to just circulate between the bed, the shower, and the toilet, but a couple of the other trainers were there, so I had to make small talk with them and keep the water use to a minimum. I noticed that as we talked, they seemed to be closely scrutinizing me, watching my face and stealing glances at my clothes. I started wondering if the road had been taking more of a toll on me than I had thought.

When I finally saw Dave that evening, his reaction to my visit seemed to be a combination of surprise and stress.

He gave me a hug and said, "Hey man, its great to see you. What on earth are you doing here?"

He was manic from last-minute preparations for the new recruits, but for a few hours we had a chance to catch up. We went on a tour of restaurants run by French expatriates, eating hamburgers and french fries in one, ice cream in another, drinking coffee in a third, beer in a fourth. He asked me about some of our fraternity brothers at home, shaking his head when I told him about all the guys in my class who had taken jobs with Procter & Gamble or Merrill Lynch. When I had last seen Dave he had been in the corporate world himself, distributing wine for Gallo out in L.A., often upset because Thunderbird and Night Train were his biggest sellers. But now he had just renewed for his third tour in the Peace Corps and he said he couldn't be happier. He was going to be one of the head trainers for a couple of years, teaching the volunteers well-digging and desert farming techniques, which they would pass on to the Malians.

He spoke Bambara and French effortlessly with the locals, joking around with the staff at each place we went. "I love West Africa," he said, "I was actually hoping you'd show up a couple of weeks ago, so I could travel around with you a bit." He said he would have loved to visit Timbuktu again and that he probably could have gotten a jeep and picked me up in Gao. Starting in the morning though, he had to be out at the training site for the next month.

Before he left, he introduced me to a few of his friends and to some of the veteran Peace Corps volunteers who were in the capital on business, or for "bush breaks." For the next five days I was in the lap of luxury, and I was able to work a bit of the travel hardship out of my system. I devoured back issues of the *International Herald Tribune* and picked up letters from home, reading all the news over and over. I did my laundry, checked on airfares to the C.A.R., and went shopping for supplies. I ate spaghetti and meatballs, cheeseburgers, M & M's, and pizza. And every evening I had dinner or went drinking with Dave's friends.

On the third night I found myself in a courtyard restaurant having a candlelit dinner with an Africare worker named Allison who had just arrived for a three-year tour setting up health programs. She was making some last-minute preparations for her work and said she had some time to kill before heading "into the bush." So we walked around town together and she helped me bargain with the merchants for some beads, change money, and plan my route onward.

I had been ready to abandon West Africa as quickly as I could, but after recharging and getting recommendations from everyone, I decided to press on by land instead of flying out. I sent a telegram home to say that I was safe and healthy and on my way to the Ivory Coast. Then I caught a ride out of Bamako with Allison the day she moved out to her post. The C.A.R. had been her first Peace Corps assignment eight years earlier, and as we drove along, she tried to encourage me with stories about how wild and fascinating it was there and in neighboring Zaire. Like most Peace Corps veterans, her musings inevitably turned to tales of strange illnesses — worms growing under her skin, lengthy stomach disorders, and brushes with death. She had been medevacked out of central Africa twice on two different Peace Corps tours — one time to Paris and the other time to Washington, D.C. All she could remember from the malarial haze of the second flight was the nurses commenting on how hairy her legs were.

"When you are out in the bush, that kind of stuff takes low priority," she said, her brown eyes wrinkling at the edges as she smiled, "and I think my dark hair made it look worse than it was." From where I sat I could see that her legs were clean shaven now under her blue-and-white sarong. Although she was nervous about her new responsibilities with Africare, she told me she was looking forward to the relative tranquility of life in Mali for a few years after the craziness of the jungle life in the C.A.R. and Gabon.

When we got close to the turnoff for the road south to the Ivory Coast, Allison suddenly asked if I wanted to go along to her village for a few days. We had not been able to stop talking each time we had been together and I had been debating for three days whether to just kiss her sometime between sentences.

We pulled over to discuss her idea and I nearly decided to go — for the fun, for the comfort, for the experience of it. But I had already honed in on Abidjan as my next destination and I was intent on covering some miles after so many days sitting still. Also, I knew that it would not make a very good impression on the villagers for her to have a man staying with her the first week — she had said as much when she originally offered me the ride. Now it was an impulsive offer, probably borne as much out of her anxiety over going off alone again as by her interest in me. I knew she would have asked sooner if it were really okay, and I also knew that while I could just move on in a few days, it was her home and her job, and she would have to overcome any negative impressions that it left with the locals. She was there for serious work, while I was just on a tour.

She looked sad and relieved at the same time when I declined. I told her that I'd better get moving if I was going to get to Zaire before the rainy season. I was hoping she'd offer to drive me to the border and stay one night with me down there, but she didn't. When she dropped me off at the road heading south toward the Ivory Coast, the wind was blowing clouds of dust and there wasn't a tree or building in sight. I gave her a kiss on the cheek and wished her great luck with her work. Then I watched her disappear down the road into the dry landscape of the Sahel.

I picked up my pack and started walking south into a headwind, feeling lonesome once again. I thought about all the miles in front of me before I got to the other side of the continent and the long weeks it would take to cover them. I couldn't even imagine how she felt heading off by herself for three years in the bush, trying somehow to build something permanent in that immutable world. Whenever you feel lonely and sorry for yourself, I thought, just remember Allison and Dave and those Peace Corps volunteers out in the sand in Mali for years at a time. Just try to remember that.

MAD DASH

IT TOOK TWO DAYS OF HITCHING and walking to reach the northern border post of the Ivory Coast. I had been told that things would be more efficient there, but I could hardly believe it when I walked out of the customs office and found air-conditioned buses ready to go to all corners of the country. Every afternoon at 4:00, they would leave all at once from the border. I had been planning to spend a few days looking around as I went south to the coast, but I couldn't resist. I hopped on the one marked "Abidjan," and took off on a blazing 400 mile overnight ride to the most modern city in West Africa.

For the first hour of the bus ride I was thrilled. We sped by villages, forests, and fields so fast that I couldn't keep track of where we were on my map. After a while, the high-backed seat began to feel uncomfortable and I had to keep turning around to get a better look through the window at a palm grove or soccer game or fruit stand we had passed. Not long after dark, after trying three different ways to sleep in the stiff seats, I found myself thinking that I would have preferred the date truck and a couple of breakdowns so that I could at least get a look at some of the village people. With me on the bus were just five Africans. Three of them wore business suits.

At about two in the morning, I was wakened by the bright orange glow of dozens of halogen lights. We were in Yamoussoukro, a town with well-paved streets, big sidewalks, and tall trees on either side. It was the president's hometown and had newly been named the capital. Beyond the trees I could see construction cranes for a nearly completed basilica that was soon to surpass St. Peter's in Rome as the largest in the world. It was being paid for entirely by the longtime president of the country with part of his immense, questionably acquired fortune. After criticism, he had announced that the basilica would be given to the Catholic Church when it was completed. Within the Church this sparked a bit of a debate that seems to have been dominated by calculated ethics. In the end, the Church announced that it would accept the offering because the good that could be done by expanding the Church in Africa far outweighed any negative stigma attached to the source. Besides, a group of bishops had said after visiting, unlike many other countries the Ivory Coast at least had paved roads and running water to show for all of the foreign investment.

When we arrived in Abidjan at dawn, it was readily apparent where the president's money had come from. It was like being in a French city — in Dijon, or perhaps Marseilles with the big harbor. There were high-rise hotels, office buildings, and apartments. There were parks and promenades and French department stores and boutiques. Wandering around with my heavy pack on, I felt out of place and a little embarrassed for the first time since I'd been in Africa. I couldn't figure out where to stay because all the hotels in the center of town were expensive international hotels. At the

Catholic mission, the nun who answered the door took one look at me and said, "Non. Complet," before shutting the door in my face.

At the Protestant mission I was treated pretty much the same way. "Sorry, all full," the woman said. When I asked her for recommendations she suggested a neighborhood on the other side of town that had accommodations in my range. I walked for half an hour and then found a room in a one-star hotel that had red lights in the corridor and hourly rates.

My plan was to get out to some of the beaches as soon as possible and then work my way along the coast through Ghana, Togo, and Benin to Nigeria, Cameroon, and then the Central African Republic. Everyone had told me great stories about beachside bungalows, twenty-five-cent pineapples, and dollar lobsters in Ghana and Togo. I was figuring that if I could get to Bangui, the capital of the C.A.R., in three weeks, then it would be well worth the extra effort of going by land. But first I had to get some visas.

I went to the Ghana embassy at eleven in the morning and was told to wait. Seven others, all Africans, were in the waiting room with me. We watched the consular go to lunch and come back and then leave again at 4:00. At 5:30 we were told that we should leave too, the office was closing. The next day, Friday, I arrived early in the morning and was told that visas were only processed on Tuesdays and Thursdays, so I should come back Tuesday. I explained that I had been there on Thursday and that I was planning to go to Ghana on Sunday and could not possibly wait until Wednesday to depart.

I left my passport and went out to get some lunch. On the way back, I stopped at the Air Afrique office and found out that flights to Bangui went every Sunday and Thursday — $350 for a nine-hour flight with three stops along the way. When I got back to the consulate office, nothing had been done and the consular was "still busy." While I sat waiting I had time to more reasonably calculate the miles and the days and the likely cost to go by land to Bangui. Almost any way I planned it, I realized that it would probably cost me five or six hundred dollars and a lot more time than three weeks to get to Bangui. I had four to six weeks before the rainy season began in Zaire, which I had been warned would make the jungle roads to East Africa extremely difficult to get through. When I asked again about my visa I was told that the consular had "gone for the day." Suddenly, flying seemed like an excellent option.

I grabbed my passport, restrained myself from completely burning bridges with the haughty woman behind the desk, and hurried over to the Air Afrique office to see if I could get a ticket for Sunday. It was closed. I hadn't noticed earlier, but the office was closed for the weekend after lunch on Fridays, as were many other stores downtown. I knew I couldn't wait until Thursday, and I figured there must be some way to get a ticket for the Sunday flight. I looked up Air Afrique in the phone book and asked someone how to use the pay phone, but a recording kept coming on that I couldn't understand. Then I checked into getting a ride out to the airport, but the taxi drivers wanted seventeen dollars and I couldn't figure out where to catch the proper bus. I found the tourist office, but that was closed too. After a couple of hours of scrambling around, it dawned on me that I could make reservations through the concierge at the Hilton. He took care of it for me in three minutes and checked to make sure that the Central African Republic visa I had gotten in Bamako was okay. All I had to do was get to the airport early enough on Sunday to pay for the ticket.

I was thrilled. Just like that, the dry Sahel of West Africa was a memory and all my thoughts turned to the equatorial jungle. The flight was going to stop in Togo, Nigeria, and Cameroon before landing in Bangui, following almost exactly the route I had planned. The thought of covering all those miles in one fell swoop was exhilarating. I tried to sit in the Hilton lobby and read the paper, but for the rest of the day I kept pulling out my maps, feeling almost intoxicated as my mind raced ahead.

On Saturday, I didn't feel quite so good about the whole thing. I woke up doubting whether I had made the right decision. I knew it made sense logically, but in my heart, I couldn't help but feel I might be compromising too much. I told myself that I didn't have to physically move across Africa just to be able to tell people back home that I had done it. But I also told myself that it wasn't for people back home that I had wanted to do it, it was for me, so that I could have a sense of the places and a sense of personal accomplishment. If I had flown over half of the Sahara, it certainly wouldn't have felt the same. But I knew I had to make a compromise someplace. If I hadn't gone to Timbuktu and Bamako, I would have been halfway through Zaire already and would not have to worry about the rains. I had been on the continent nearly two months, and I was just beginning to head east. If I got hung up getting through each little country along the coast, then I could end up spending eight months just getting to Kenya and never make it the rest of the way around the world.

All morning and afternoon I sat in the air-conditioned lobby of the Sheraton and read the *International Herald Tribune* and the *London Times*. I had thought about trying to get out to the coastal beaches for the day, but I didn't have the energy. I found out which buses to take to the airport and wrote some letters home. I gave my family the American Express address for Nairobi where I hoped to be in a month or a month and-a-half and tried to estimate my route across equatorial Africa as best as I could. I promised to write regularly, but my Peace Corps friends had told me that Zaire would be the "real Africa," with no paved roads and very little infrastructure. Letters from there, I warned my folks, could take a month or longer to get to the States.

When I got back to my hotel that night, I reorganized my pack and went to bed early so that I would be sure to get to the airport on time. I couldn't sleep, though, first because I kept thinking about Zaire, and then because I was repeatedly wakened by loud noises in the hallway and nearby rooms as the hourly customers came and went.

Finally at 6:30 AM, I gave up trying to sleep and walked into town to get a little breakfast and catch the bus to the airport. I arrived two and a half hours before my flight, feeling nervous and excited, as if I were starting my trip all over again. It was the earliest I'd ever been for a flight, but it wasn't early enough. When I tried to pay for my ticket at the Air Afrique counter, they told me they could not accept a credit card.

"Only at the city office," the African woman behind the counter explained to me in French.

I checked my cash and traveler's checks. I was $140 short. No problem, I thought, I can get into town, get the ticket and get back in time. But then, when I got outside, I remembered that it was Sunday — everything was still closed.

I went back to the counter and the woman said, "Yes, of course, the office is closed today."

I stared at her for a few seconds, took a deep breath and then put all the money that I had on the counter. "Is it possible to charge only $140?" I tried to ask in French.

"No," she said, "No charge." The supervisor said the same thing, as well as the next person who came out. In their green uniforms and multicolored scarves, they looked like regular, everyday, friendly airline attendants, but they didn't offer any suggestions, or seem very concerned at all.

"Are there any other possibilities?" I asked, starting to feel the reality sinking in and the panic rising.

They looked at each other and around the airport and shrugged. "There is another flight on Thursday," one of them said. They all nodded. I imagined the calendar days passing page by page while I grew old in the red-light hotel, or the waiting room of the Ghana consulate.

I turned and looked around the small airport. It was one big room on the bottom floor with airline desks and a couple of car rental stands. Upstairs there was a cafeteria and some offices.

I tried to think calmly and clearly, to lay out my options. I had an hour and forty-five minutes. I went to the Avis counter and pulled out my Gold Card and asked for help. They looked at me like I was crazy. So did the people at the small Air France desk and at Alitalia.

"Perhaps another passenger could help you," the man in the airport manager's office said after I waited fifteen minutes to see him. "I'm sorry, there is nothing I can do if you don't have money."

The restaurant manager was more sympathetic. He agreed that it might by a good thing if Air Afrique accepted credit cards at the airport, and he offered me a coffee and roll on the house. I was trying to come up with an appropriate response when I heard a boarding call for my flight. My watch said 10:30, forty-five minutes until takeoff. My heart sank. I scanned the airport again and considered my options. Part of me said, "Just give up, head out to the beaches, and come back in a few days," but another part kept insisting, "There must be a way — just find it."

I thought about selling my camera, but who would I sell it to? There were twenty-five or thirty Europeans in the airport, but none of them looked like they needed a camera, and I didn't want to travel without mine anyway. Just ask one of them for help, I thought. In Africa, there was a consistent bond between the whites, kind of similar to the easy bond between blacks in America. We would always say hello to each other in the cities and would stop and have lengthy conversations if paths crossed in a remote area. Only in nice hotels and in airports, it seemed, did the rule not hold. But surely some of these fellow travelers would respond to someone in need, I thought, especially if I could find an American.

I approached a few people near the booths downstairs and briefly tried to tell them my situation. Each practically ran away — probably as much from my bad French as from what they thought I might be saying. I canvassed the restaurant upstairs and introduced myself to an American family from Texas. I tried to play it cool and not seem desperate.

"I can write you a check from my Shearson Lehman account," I said to the man, hoping he would be impressed. "I have more than enough in there and the account automatically covers bounces anyway."

I could tell he believed me and I thought for a second he would bite. He clearly had the money. His kids had been staring, wide-eyed, and he smiled at them to reassure them, but his wife was horrified. She looked as if a homeless person had hopped into her limo. One glance at her ruined my chances.

"Umm, I'd really like to help you out," he said, "but have you tried Air France or Lufthansa?"

I nodded. "I know its a weird request," I said, "but it'll cost me nearly a week if I don't make this flight, so I thought it was worth trying." His wife nervously started getting the kids together to go.

"I'm sorry," he said, "I just can't. I'm sorry."

"Thanks for considering it," I said, feeling like an idiot.

"Good luck," he said sincerely. I could tell that he felt as bad as I did. Everyone in the restaurant was looking over at us as I picked up my bags to go.

I decided to give up. I felt sick to my stomach from the embarrassing rushing around and the disappointment. Perhaps this is a sign that flying was a bad choice, I thought to myself, just bite the bullet and go by land. Almost instantly the realization of the distance between Abidjan and Bangui, and the obstacles in covering those 1,800 miles began to weigh on me. Oh, God! I thought.

As I walked back down the stairs, I noticed that there were agents at the Swissair counter who had not been there before. I half-heartedly asked if they could process a credit card advance. The woman behind the counter asked a couple of questions about the details and then surprised me by being entirely sympathetic. She swung into action like she was part of a trauma team. We ran upstairs to their office where she called France twice and then telexed three times before getting an approval from American Express. The whole time, I had been watching the clock and listening to the final boarding calls for my flight come and go. It was 11:15.

"I'm afraid it's too late," I said as the telex was printing out. "We will see," she said. Then she and her supervisor took the telex to the Air Afrique desk and demanded that they give me my ticket and let me board. The gate was closed, the baggage inspectors had left and I thought I could hear the jet engines revving. I was sure there was going to be a big flap, and I began to wonder if I might have made too big a deal out of the whole thing, if maybe I should have been a little more African in my attitude and just rolled with the punches and gone off in search of pineapples and lobsters for a few days.

But to my complete amazement, the previously implacable Air Afrique agents did exactly as they were told. It took them ten minutes to process my ticket and they held the plane for me. They had to wheel the stairs back into position and reopen the door as I ran across the tarmac with my backpack. I was so relieved as I settled into my seat, sweating and breathing heavily, that I was only a little embarrassed by the stares of my fellow passengers. About half the people in the plane were those I had gone to for help, and most of them looked appalled that I was on the plane with them. But one older woman I didn't recognize applauded softly and gave me a respectful nod and a big smile. At least someone was pulling for me, I thought as I settled into my seat. I had the moral suasion of the Swiss and one good fan.

She's probably Swiss too, I mused, or maybe Danish — perhaps a long-lost relative of Isak Dinesen or an old friend of Beryl Markham.

As the plane rumbled and jumped from slow taxi to full throttle takeoff, my heart jumped too. I watched Abidjan shrink and saw the white beaches and the white foaming breakers as we banked toward the east. I ate two big, Western-style meals between stopovers in Lomé, Lagos, and Douala, and savored every sight along the way. As we flew out of Cameroon on the last leg to Bangui, I could see the rain-forest canopy so thick and green that it looked like someone could walk on it. I couldn't believe it could exist so close to the Sahara. As we climbed higher, the view was obscured for a few seconds and then we could see the sun shining again on a sea of whiteness. I smiled, thinking of the times as a kid that I had wanted to float on fluffy clouds like those. And then I smiled even broader with the realization that they were the first clouds I had seen in nearly two months.

THE CONGO

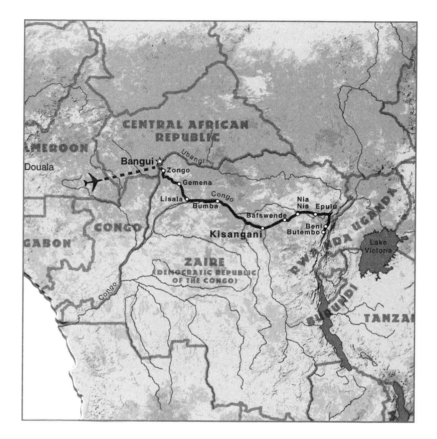

The offing was barred by a black bank of clouds, and the tranquil waterway leading to the uttermost ends of the earth flowed somber under an overcast sky — seemed to lead into the heart of an immense darkness.

JOSEPH CONRAD

SOLDIERS' PLAYGROUND

IN BANGUI, THE CAPITAL of the Central African Republic, only the heat rules. Because the city rests just five degrees north of the equator, even in February all work is done in the morning to avoid the brutal afternoon sun. Banks are open from 6:30 AM to 1:00 PM, and stores generally follow the same hours. Still, the heat makes things crazy. The country as a whole tends to be chaotic, with one of the most tumultuous political histories in modern Africa. Time and again, the French Special Forces have had to move into their old colony to stabilize things. But even the stable times have an undercurrent of wildness.

As I walked through Bangui on the morning of February 13, I could feel an almost kinetic difference from the sleepier, easier-going West Africa. When I stopped at the gate of the Presidential mansion, not realizing what it was, a French Foreign Legion soldier

carrying a machine gun came out of the guard booth and demanded to see my passport. Fortunately, I had it with me. The
palace, I later found out, was a place where the notorious
"Emperor" Bokassa had once thrown enemies into a lion pit.
Others he supposedly cannibalized. A huge soccer stadium nearby
stood empty because no one had the heart to use it after a hundred
children had been murdered there in the late seventies by
Bokassa's troops. There was not enough money to tear it down, but
the jungle was already reclaiming it. Trees were growing up
through the stands. Vegetation engulfed the playing field, showing
bright green through the dark stadium tunnels.

In Bangui, French and Belgian merchants seemed to control
every product, from food to hardware to gasoline. They all seethed
with disdain for the Africans and the tourists (and each other for
that matter). Each of them was so volatile that just going into
their stores and buying soap felt like a dangerous adventure, and I
wondered if some of them were former soldiers who had come
back to their old post. Monkeys were the pet of choice in this
crowd, who would walk and drive around town with the little animals sitting on their shoulders. And no matter what store they
ran, these merchants were all in the diamond business in some
way, closing up at a whim to run off in their white jeeps in search
of an easy fortune.

The African locals, meanwhile, sold beautiful trinkets and col-
orfully dyed clothes and small piles of fruits and vegetables at stalls
in the common market. They labored during the day at the shops
and homes of the expatriate merchants. At night the most ambitious studied under the streetlights, while others danced until all
hours at the numerous thatch-roofed, cinder block clubs. Everywhere I went, I could hear central African "congo music" with its
driving bassline and repetitive, synthesized steel-drum refrains.

The Peace Corps workers in West Africa had told me again and
again that the C.A.R. Peace Corps had the lowest morale and was
considered the worst post that could be drawn, not just in Africa,

but throughout the world. I had not intended to seek out the volunteers there, but because the Catholic mission was charging fifteen dollars a night for a room, and the city campground had a platoon of guards armed with bows and arrows trying to ward off thieves, I ended up again at the Peace Corps hostel. Surprisingly, the volunteers there were in much better spirits than their Malian counterparts. They seemed to relish the hardship and wildness of their post, telling story after story of hunting trips and cooking lessons and strange initiation rights in their villages. At the time, their administrators were trying to figure out how to deal with one rogue volunteer who had adopted native dress and face paint and was refusing to come in from his post for a scheduled vacation.

Most of them took a great interest in my trip and at night, over large bottles of Primus beer, they helped me plan for my journey through Zaire. I went to the American embassy to register my route and get the latest reports on Zaire, Rwanda, Tanzania, and some of the other countries that I was thinking about traveling through. As usual, I had to go through three security checkpoints at the embassy, with local security guards on the outside and U.S. Marines on the inside. But at least this time I got to speak to an American once I got inside — and with no bulletproof glass between us. The young State Department official told me the same thing that the volunteers had: "Try to get through the Zaire jungle before the rains come, and be careful about paying bribes. Pay as little as possible, make it clear that you think it is a fee, and don't do anything to make it worth their trouble to detain you." The political conditions along the way were pretty stable compared to what they had been a few years before, he told me, but in the eastern areas of the country, rebel uprisings were always a possibility. If anything erupted, he said, lay low, get in touch with the nearest consulate, and don't get involved.

"No problem," I said, "I'm just going through as quick as I can."

"There's no such thing as 'no problem,'" he said dryly. And I laughed because I thought he was making a joke rather than summarizing his views on Africa in general.

Later that afternoon, I was walking through the quiet streets, trying to stay on the shady side, when a couple of the Peace Corps workers and one of the marines from the embassy pulled up next to me in a small American Jeep. They had beach towels with them and asked if I wanted to go swimming. I hopped in the back and we sped through town and then along the Ubangi River until the houses thinned out. I assumed we were going to find a quiet spot on the river, and I tried to keep from thinking about crocodiles and piranhas which I had read were common in the vicinity. But instead, we pulled up at a long, ranch-style house surrounded by palm trees and a big hedge. It was the home of the marine guards.

When I realized where we were, at first I felt a little apprehensive, though I'm not sure why. Hanging out in Africa with Peace Corps volunteers was one thing, but marines seemed like another — a little too close to home, perhaps, to be legitimate. And sure enough, their place was almost like being back in the States. When we walked in, two of the marines were microwaving frozen pizzas and another two were on the sectional sofa watching taped soap operas on a wide-screen TV. They were cordial but not friendly. We could eat their food if we liked, play pool or video games, go swimming and sunbathing out back, even take a shower — just as long as we didn't try to actually have a conversation.

Outside, all of the Peace Corps volunteers I had met in the hostel were arrayed around the pool, tanning on a deck that overlooked the river and the northern border of Zaire beyond. The whole scene was so incongruous with the rest of Bangui that it felt decadent and frivolously fun. The pool was good-sized, clean, blue, and cold because they were constantly adding fresh water. There was a real grass lawn around the deck, something I hadn't seen in a while, and palm trees scattered about. Surrounding everything was a high, hedge-lined, barbed-wire fence, with African security guards circling every ten or fifteen minutes to check that everything was intact. Docked down below, on our side of the river, was a speedboat, which the marines used for water-skiing when the water was high enough.

But now the river was low, with rocks showing everywhere. While I relaxed on a chaise lounge, I looked down at the river, trying to see where I would have to cross, wishing some other travelers were going to be heading into Zaire with me. On my third day back at the pool, some of the volunteers started asking me when I planned to leave. I'd been talking to everyone about every nuance of my next leg for five days. Now my visas were set for Zaire, Rwanda, Tanzania, Kenya, and even Uganda if I decided to go that way.

"I guess I'm going tomorrow," I said, feeling an overwhelming sense of dread just in saying it. I felt entirely weakened by the luxury of the ranch house, and by the luxury of having taken the flight, and the modern amenities of Abidjan, and even by the wonderful company in Bamako and Bangui. Instead of building me up, it all seemed to have stripped me down and made me needy, void of willpower. After three months of travel, the thought of setting off again into the unknown had begun to seem awful. I wanted to insulate myself from Africa and pretend I was home, like the marines did, staying clean and well-fed and unencumbered by the hardships of the people around them.

My last night in Bangui, we all went to a dance club and I drank too much and overslept the next morning. I wanted to just stay in bed, but I got up anyway and packed my things. I gave a letter and a small package for my family to a volunteer who was returning to Kansas and was going to mail them for me when she got home. Then I grabbed some lunch and headed down to the river.

ANOTHER WORLD

AN OLD MAN WHO HAD NO TEETH and looked to me like an African Charon ferried me across the river to the border post at Zongo in a long pirogue. On the other side, three customs officials were waiting like Cerebus, each of them salivating as I came up the hill. They asked for a 15,000 zaire entrance fee, which was forty dollars, but I worked my way out of it by telling them that I was in the Peace Corps and was on my way to Bukavu for training. The volunteers in Bangui had told me to say this because the head customs man was a Christian who was very much in favor of the Peace Corps' work and felt guilty about pushing the volunteers to give bribes. I had to say a lot more, too, pretending not to understand them sometimes and insisting that the government had exempted all Peace Corps members from the entrance fee by special embassy arrangements. Finally, they wore down and let me go on through.

I got a ride in the back of a truck that went 125 miles southeast over dirt roads to Gemena, the capital of the northern region.
I was fascinated by the eerie beauty of the land. There were thousands and thousands of palm trees, open spaces with tall green grass
and white cattails, rolling tan and green and deep brown hum-
mocks. Much of the land looked perfect for building and farming,
especially compared to the Sahel, but hardly anyone was there.

When I got off the truck in Gemena, I was standing in the
small town square, trying to figure out where I might pitch my
tent, when an older African man approached me and asked if I
needed a place to stay. When he realized that I didn't speak
French very well, he switched to English. He said that he stayed
at the Catholic mission just down the street and that they would
be happy to have me there. I thought we had made a deal to pitch
my tent in their yard, but when we got there he showed me to a
large room that faced onto a courtyard that was part of the mission school. He insisted that I join him for dinner and then introduced himself before leaving. His name was Bishop Antoine, and
later, when I joined him to eat, he told me that he was the bishop
of the diocese of Gemena which covered all of northwestern
Zaire. He had been educated at the Sorbonne and the Vatican,
and was impeccably mannered.

The two of us had dinner on a screened-in porch behind his
house, complete with beer, chicken, plantains, a pretty close ap-
proximation of French bread, tea, and fresh pineapples for dessert.
It was a little difficult for us to converse, in a mixture of French
and English, but we had a nice conversation nonetheless, each of
us guessing a bit at what the other was saying. Things had been
very quiet lately, he told me, because the rivers were way down
and the trucks could not be ferried across. This time of year they
always felt cut off from the rest of the country.

Things were peaceful in Zaire, he told me, but not very good.
Many people were struggling to get by, while President Mobutu did
everything he could to create a sense of national unity that would

reach across all the different tribal divisions. Bishop Antoine felt caught in the middle between the politicians and the people, unable to really help either cause. He believed that only massive European and American aid could create the infrastructure and base resources necessary to get a viable, unifying economy going.

I asked him about some of the stories I had heard about Mobutu's excessive and growing wealth — his villas on the Riviera and his Swiss bank accounts — but he said he did not know about any of that. As he drank more beer, he spoke more in French, so that by the end of the meal, as the sun set outside, he was speaking entirely in a fluid, elegant French with me nodding and catching only every fifth or sixth word.

In the morning we had tea, fruit, and croissants before he sent me on my way with a letter of introduction to use at Catholic missions between there and Lisala. I'm set now, I thought. But the letter was taken away by the local police before I even left town, and this time the "registration fee" was obligatory. Fortunately, it was just a few dollars.

I spent the rest of the day in the back of a loaded flatbed truck going a hundred miles further southeast to Akula on the banks of the Mongala River. We arrived at dusk and there were hundreds of people camped up and down the streets, waiting for the water to rise enough to get their goods across. It was a wild scene, with music and drinking and small fires scattered everywhere. On the other side of the river, it appeared to be very quiet, but at that hour, I couldn't find anyone to paddle me across.

I set up my tent next to a small crowd of raucous men and women on the sandy boat landing. They seemed to have been there for days, drinking all the while. When I went to relieve myself in the middle of the night, they started yelling to me and asking me things I couldn't understand. One of them wanted me to have a drink with them, so I sat down and accepted a warm beer, trying to be cordial while a heavy, toothless woman tried to work her way onto my lap. They were friendly, but a few of them had a menacing edge that made me wary. Though they looked like they had little money, they all started asking to buy my shoes, my watch, my camera, and anything else of value that I had along. I did my best to keep things light, laughing and pretending that they were just kidding, even when a couple of the men got belligerent about their demands.

After an exhausting half hour, I said thanks and goodnight and tried to move coolly to my tent. The toothless woman saw me though, and tried to crawl in with me. One of the men, who called her his sister, seemed particularly supportive of the idea, but I told her again and again that she was too much of a woman for me, and that I was married and shy and too tired. They all laughed uproariously at this and I just played off their laughter until she finally left.

When she came back again a little later, the few people still awake did not seem inclined to laugh about it anymore. But I pretended that I was too sleepy to understand. I was sure that someone would try to take some of my things during the night and I was worried that they might come after me too. I got out my knife, but then put it back in my pocket, knowing that with so many of them, it would only make any situation worse.

For the first half of the night I barely slept at all, and lay awake listening to their Lingala conversation. Eventually they all quieted down and I was able to doze off. The rest of the night I had terrible dreams and toward morning I was awakened by a large pig routing around outside my tent, the noises half incorporated into my nightmares. It was the woman with no teeth and then a lion and then a ferocious dog ready to rip through the tent. Finally the pig was so noisy that I woke up, packed up my stuff, and went down by the water to wait for a canoe.

In the morning, Akula seemed like a different place. It was quiet and the river dominated the landscape. The water was a couple hundred yards across, with big rocks exposed everywhere in the riverbed. A few fishermen were casting nets from their pirogues in the shallow water. On the southern side, I could see a few huts and some people pulling their boats down. On the northern side where I was, people were sleeping all around on the ground and skinny dogs had joined the rogue pig sniffing about for scraps.

I made some tea on my little stove and ate some bread and jelly that was left over from the Catholic mission. Eventually, a couple of teenagers came poling across in their dugout pirogue and ferried me back with them. On the other side, there were bunches of manioc leaves, bananas, cola nuts, and a few tiny vegetables laid out on the beach for sale. A handful of people who lived there were getting ready for their day, mending nets, sweeping in front of their huts, arranging their wares to sell to the occasional traveler.

I bought some bananas and walked down the road a short way to look around for trucks or a café where I could wait for a ride. There was nothing. The road ended right at the river, and since the large ferries could not get any trucks across, I had to wait for a driver to come up from the southeast, where I was going, and then turn around to go back. I tried to ask some of the locals if they expected any trucks, but no one spoke French or English. They understood where I wanted to go, though, since there was only one road, and they motioned for me to wait. So I waited. I found a chair on the veranda of an empty store and pulled out Isak Dinesen's *Out Of Africa,* one of the new books I had traded for at the hostel in Bangui.

At first a small crowd hung around watching me, but eventually they got bored and left — all but one skinny kid who stayed for hours just staring at me. When I tried to talk to him, his eyes grew wider, but he would not respond, except for an occasional tiny smile. After a bit, he took to lying down on crossrails of the fence that was in front of me, one arm straight up to hold onto the rail above him, the other arm dangling straight down, as if he'd been crucified sideways. His constant stare was a little disconcerting at first, but once I got used to it, he was good company.

Unfortunately, because it was hot, I drank a lot more water than I normally would in a new place, and by noon I was starting to feel queasy. I had treated the local well water with my iodine tablets as usual, but I hadn't given my system enough time to adjust to it. For the next three hours I had to run into the jungle every twenty minutes, then every ten minutes to relieve myself. The flies would swarm instantly and were so aggressive that I had to keep moving during the process. Most of what I left behind was gone even before I came back again. I felt thoroughly disgusted and while I was cursing and swatting at the flies, my little friend would watch from the road, wide-eyed.

"You know, there is really no need for you to follow me *every* time I go to the bathroom," I said to him in English at one point when I felt particularly worn out by the ordeal. "It's the same routine every time. Don't you have some homework to do or something?"

Of course he couldn't understand a word I was saying, but he blinked at me and left. I felt bad until he came back a little while later with a water pitcher for me — the kind that many Africans use to wash with instead of toilet paper. I was not fond of the technique, but I was touched by the gesture and I made sure I took it with me the next time I ran into the jungle.

Midafternoon a truck finally came, already loaded with goods and apparently looking for passengers. I was the only one waiting in that village, but it wasn't long before we picked up a few more along the road, walking with huge bundles on their heads in what seemed like the middle of nowhere. They would nod at the others as they climbed up top, and then stare straight ahead as we bounced along the rough roads through the lush and rugged terrain. When I got some of them to talk to me, they were very pleased to know that I was from the U.S. Two of the men told me that they wanted to join the U.S. Army because it had the best fighters in the world and paid well. They knew this, they said, from friends who had trained with the Americans in the southern part of the country, near the Angolan border. I was struck by their intensity and aggressiveness. Violence was not out of the question with them as it had seemed to be in the Sahel. They clearly were less peaceful, less easygoing than the West Africans, as if the world somehow sat heavier with them. I could only hope that Americans had not helped make it so.

Fortunately, my stomach settled down during the long ride and I was feeling much better by the time we stopped for the night in dormitories at an old coffee and rubber plantation near Mitoko. It was a huge plantation with its own network of roads and numerous trucks and jeeps running about. I was told that the Belgians still owned the plantation, but that their presence had been greatly reduced by President Mobutu's policies. The next morning I saw the main house and some of the processing buildings. They all had the sloping verandas and the weathered white columns of the colonial era. A few white men, who I assumed were Belgians, passed our truck that morning, honking and cursing as they went. They wore khaki suits and arrogant scowls, and except for their Toyota or Mercedes jeeps, they seemed to have stepped out of the old days of the Belgian Congo. Despite Mobutu's efforts to Africanize the nation, vestiges of colonialism were clearly still in place. Most of the trappings were gone, but foreigners still owned and ran many of the big companies.

Not far from the plantation, the air got hazy and acrid. We soon crossed through miles of charred landscape where rainforest had recently been burned to create more fields for coffee, rubber plants, and date palms. Many of the stumps were still smoking, creating an eerie, otherworldly setting. The scene was duplicated through the day as we headed east towards Lisala, passing only occasionally through tiny villages where worn-looking people huddled in their doorways and stared at us as we passed.

It was after dark when we finally got to Lisala, where I planned to catch a boat up the old Congo River (which Mobutu had renamed the Zaire). The town, with its combination of colo-

nial, cinder block, and thatched-roof buildings, sat on a bluff overlooking the enormous river. From the hill at night, the Congo was
just a black void beyond the trees, making me feel as if I'd come
to the end of the earth. We parked the truck in front of the old
colonial hotel and as soon as the engine was turned off, I could
hear the chirping and buzzing of the night jungle. Moths and
other bugs gathered on the hotel screens in the soft, orange light
and tinny strains of music came from within. I went inside with
the three drivers and joined them for a dinner of peanuts, beer,
and greasy fish. My drivers were the only Africans eating there.
The place was stripped of its colonial splendor and most of the
clients were scruffy travelers, including some German hippies who
had come in a VW van, and two guys from Denmark who had just
arrived on motorcycles. All of them were camping in the yard instead of staying in the dingy rooms, so after dinner I put up my
tent outside and joined the club of people who were waiting for
the boat to Kisangani, already four days overdue.

RIVER OF STARS

THE NEXT MORNING I was told that it would be at least another day before the boat came, maybe longer. Nobody had to tell me what that meant. I looked around for another place to stay because the hotel scene was too noisy and I wanted to be down by the river. I felt drawn to it, and for the first time since Europe, I wanted to stay a bit apart from the other tourists. I found an old hotel by the river that had eight rooms, six of which were occupied by the family that ran it. From the way the children acted, I think I was the first non-African to ever come by. Whenever I was in the room during the day, the kids would check frequently through the hole in the wall that served as a window to see what I was doing. Sometimes they would just lean in on the windowsill and watch me reading or writing.

The room had cinder block walls with the single window, a large bed, and an old wooden desk. The first night, in the dim candlelight, I saw a large bug on the wall and when I looked closer I realized that it was a scorpion, its tail curled up, just hanging out on the wall like a spider. I kept tabs on it for a couple of hours, but it didn't move very much, so I left it and in the morning it was still there. When I asked the owner about it, he said it wasn't a problem. But he didn't want to touch it either. We both knew that if we didn't get it on the first hit, it would come after us. There were also mosquitoes and bedbugs, so the second night I put my tent up on the bed and slept inside it.

Of course the kids loved this. They seemed to think that most everything I did was pretty amusing: my constant writing, the hours I kept, all the bananas and peanuts I ate, the way I kept staring out at the river. From my window I could see glimpses of water through the trees, but I could feel its proximity even when I wasn't looking, and I would frequently go down and watch its movements. At Lisala, the Zaire River was at least a half a mile across, muddy and deep — by far the biggest river I had ever seen. All day and all night an enormous volume of water kept pushing past, clumps of vegetation continually floating by as if there had just been a huge storm upriver. The current was so strong that it felt as if the water were grumbling as it coursed by, beating out a rhythm in the eddies with its relentless westward flow. It seemed that if you fell in, you wouldn't be able to get out until you reached Kinshasa, over six hundred miles southwest, or the ocean nearly four hundred miles beyond that. But I wasn't planning to go with the current. I wanted to go three hundred miles upriver, almost straight east along the equator to Kisangani, and then by land through the dense jungle of the Ituri Forest beyond that.

Near the dock where the boats that ran between Kinshasa and Kisangani were supposed to come in four times a week, there was a little market that sold fruits, vegetables, fish, and various other goods that the boats would bring. There were local pastries for a penny or three cents each and I found a tea stall that brewed some local leaves together with sweet milk to create an irresistible concoction that sometimes drew me back three times in a day. With the tea I would eat fresh bread covered with local peanut butter, and in the morning I especially liked to sit and watch the bustle of the women setting up their stands. They would arrive with baskets full of produce on their heads, and laugh, gossip, and barter relentlessly with each other, stopping only for the 7:30 AM flag-raising ceremony, complete with recorded music that would crackle out over the river while the women yawned.

I bought avocados, onions, tomatoes, garlic, and red hot peppers and made a "Congo guacamole" that had me breathing fire for days. The boat kept being delayed and I wrote and read and eventually cleaned up all my gear, giving my tent, my backpack, and my clothes much-needed washings. The owner of the hotel would come by each day with fresh candles, and outside my window a little old man who appeared to be the sole employee was constantly sweeping the dirt yard to keep it free of any vegetation. As he worked he whistled the same languid phrase over and over again, as if he were a bird. He was responsible for keeping buckets of fresh water outside my room, but when I saw him struggling with the buckets one day a quarter mile from the hotel, I began to insist that I get the water myself. In the late afternoon when I finished writing, after the heat had permeated everything, I would pour the buckets over my head in the breezeway and then sit by the river and let the warm wind dry me.

In the evenings I walked up the hill to get some food and check in with the ever-growing gang of tourists at the big hotel. To put their cars on the riverboats, everyone had to catch the boat either in Lisala or at Bumba, sixty miles further east. It was the only real route through the center of the continent and everyone was funneled to this one area. They were all worried about getting across the jungle before the rains came, each day lamenting when the boat failed to arrive. I was anxious about it coming too, but each day when the official report came up "not until tomorrow," I found that I was content to stay a little longer.

At night, the electricity was usually shut off throughout the town, so the big hotel was lit only by gas lanterns and candles. People would gather on the screened-in porch, drinking thirty-cent Zairian beers and trading stories about their journeys. Almost all of them had driven across the Sahara in jeeps or VWs or on motorcycles, and had experienced breakdowns and bribes and bad roads in Nigeria, Chad, and Cameroon. I quizzed them about the places I had missed by flying, and they made me feel better about my route by quizzing me about Timbuktu and Niger and the Ivory Coast, envious that I had gotten to see so much of West Africa. Though many of them were seasoned travelers, I soon began to realize that by traveling alone and hitching as I went, I was getting to experience more of Africa than most. Many of them seemed to be simply gunning for the next place, entirely focused on the destination. While I had certainly been guilty of that too, I realized that quite a few of them, by traveling in their own cars with their own friends, had obviously kept themselves pretty insulated from the African world they were passing through.

On the fourth night it was well after midnight when I wandered down to my place after drinking a few beers at the big hotel. The stars were out, filling the sky, but there was no moon. In the darkness of the river, clumps of vegetation continued to float by, but it was impossible to judge their scale, whether the pieces were as small as banana bunches or as big as huts. On many of the clumps there were little pieces of phosphorescence that glowed like silver fireflies — thousands of them passing down the river. It looked like a galaxy in itself, floating by and melding with the real stars until it felt as if the land were moving rather than the water. Everything was swirling in a wash of stars. I watched the landscape moving for a long while. And then I went inside to check on my scorpion, put up my clean tent, and crawl in for the night.

CONGO BOAT

WHEN THE BOAT FINALLY CAME on the morning of my sixth day in Lisala, everyone was ready. They had radioed ahead the night before that they were coming and when they rounded the bend downriver, the whole town was on the landing to greet them. The sun was shining and bright colors flashed everywhere as men and women rushed to pile their goods by the river's edge. The eighteen tourists who had been waiting in Lisala were there also, standing off to the side nervously watching their belongings, or weaving their cars through the crowd to join the queue of vehicles. We all had tickets that we had bought for the three-day journey, most of them deck passage at three dollars a day rather than the seven dollars a day for air-conditioned first-class cabins. Both tickets included meals, but the first-class meals were in a dining room rather than a slop line on the deck. I went for the deck passage, not able to resist the opportunity to save a little money and wanting to have the full experience of this Congo boat ride.

I chose poorly. The boat was the wildest, dirtiest, most chaotic operation I had ever seen. And it was actually six boats, not one. The main engine boat was a double-decker paddle steamer with the captain's quarters, first-class passenger cabins, dining room, and the wheelhouse. In front of this, lashed securely, there was another double-decker boat, then a two-story barge, and three single-level barges, tied two on one side and one on the other. Each of the barges and all of the passageways were crowded with vendors selling every product available in Zaire — toothpaste, soap, clothes, fish, fruits, vegetables, beer, car parts, batteries, radios, live and dead monkeys, goats, pigs, even crocodiles. It was a floating shopping mall. It was almost impossible to steer and the captain smashed up the dock and a few trees when he landed. With all that weight, it was pretty obvious why the boat was having engine trouble.

The crew started making room for the cars on one of the low barges as I wound my way through the crowd of people bartering goods and up to the top of the two-story barge where some of the other tourists had settled. For a while I didn't want to move, worried about leaving my gear alone. I stayed up top for a few hours watching all the commotion. But when the boat got underway, things calmed down a bit and I took a walk around with some of the others.

It was exhilarating to be out on the river, the muddy water and the piles of vegetation rushing by, the open sky above us and nothing but thick green trees on either side. African Beat music blared from three or four different saloons on board. Monkeys grabbed at my hair and clothes as I walked by. Saleswomen pushed their goods. Baton-wielding policemen cruised the passageways, not speaking to anyone except to cough out an order or ask for something from one of the vendors. Everywhere there was garbage and dirt, and the smells ranged from merely offensive to nauseating.

By three in the afternoon, I was with the rest of the tourists trying to escape the heat in the first-class dining room, drinking cold beer and signing up for the better dinner that evening. The few remaining first-class cabins were taken before the boat left the dock, but for a couple of dollars extra, the rest of us could get in on some of their meals. First class, of course, was a relative term, in this case meaning about a one-star level on the European scale. The rooms were sparse, the air-conditioning marginal, and the food poorly cooked. But compared to deck passage, it was elegant.

As the three-day trip stretched into eight days because of engine troubles, there were quite a few times that I wished I had sprung for the seven dollars a day, but as the days passed, like most of the deck tourists, I spent less and less time back in the first-class section. Surprisingly, most of the cabin crowd started spending time up front with us, even in the middle of the day. Like New York City, once the initial shock wore off, the chaotic atmosphere of the boat became appealing, and the first-class food and beer ran out by the fourth day anyway, so they were soon eating the same food as the rest of us. Somehow the stewed fish heads and rice came to seem more palatable eaten out of a beat-up cooking tin on the barge roof than eaten from chipped china with stained linens and mismatched silverware.

In Bumba, on the third day, we picked up three more barges so that the boat had nine pieces lashed together, three across. We also picked up fifteen more tourists, bringing the total to over thirty. Their VWs and Land Rovers and Citroëns were hoisted with a crane onto the upper deck of the barge where we were camped out. I was sure one of them would be dropped, but they were safely added to our tent city, with tarps running between the vehicles and tents scattered about. People settled into playing harmonicas and guitars, and checkers and backgammon. They drank all afternoon and evening and talked about everything imaginable. There were now travelers from Denmark, Holland, Belgium,

Germany, France, England, Canada, Japan, Australia, New Zealand, and America, including another American who was also traveling on his own. Just making the rounds could take up the whole day.

The one Canadian was tall, bearded, in his late twenties, with the wrinkles of a forty-year-old and the disposition of a teenager. He had been traveling since he finished college six years earlier, stopping every once in a while to make money: coaching hockey in New Zealand, playing semi-pro basketball in Taiwan, teaching English in Japan. Along the way, he had studied martial arts, stayed in Buddhist monasteries, and visited Hindu ashrams. He had also tried to expand his mind with every drug he could get his hands on. He wanted to achieve enlightenment in this life, he told me, and he had been "making good progress" until he came to Africa. While on the boat he spent most of his time drinking beer and playing backgammon, though occasionally he did climb up onto one of the rooftops and sit in a lotus position facing the sun as it sank into the wide river.

Two of the Australians were women in their early twenties who had bought an old Land Rover in Germany, had crossed the Sahara in Algeria, and then driven from Niger into Chad, Cameroon, and the C.A.R. They looked like most of the cheerleaders I had known in high school, except that they always had grease on their faces and under their nails from working on their truck. When they left home, they said, they hadn't even known how to change the oil. But they had figured that out before leaving Italy — and now they could clean the fuel lines and filters, replace the carburetor and brakes, rework the suspension if necessary. They were planning to go all the way to South Africa if the truck held out, or at least to Tanzania. "I'll never be the same if I get through this," one of them told me. I think she was pleased about that.

The one Japanese guy was very shy and would only communicate with a German woman who had gained his confidence. He had biked all the way from Norway, through the Sahara, and then to a little village near Bumba. There he had traded his bike for some local artwork because he knew he could not pedal through the Zaire jungle before the rains came. But as the days went by on the boat, he became more and more reclusive until one morning we realized that he was gone. During the night, his German friend told us, he had bought a canoe from one of the locals in the Go Beer Bar, and then set out back downriver to repurchase his bike. His goal had been to cycle from Norway to South Africa, and he believed he could live with the hardship of biking through the rainy season easier than the failure of going by boat and car. His effort was frequently toasted the rest of the week.

Throughout the trip the engines on the boats kept breaking. Sometimes the captain would pull up along the bank to rearrange them so that the working engines were in the back. He would string the barges out for a half a mile along the shore and then come by and reconnect one by one. When all the engines were down we would have to anchor until a couple of them were fixed. In the daytime it was pretty rough to be without the breeze that the movement gave, but at night it was a little cooler. We would sit up on the deck and watch the local villagers paddling out in their pirogues loaded with goods. Sometimes we didn't see any people or towns for fifty miles, but when we were anywhere near one, men and women would chase the boat and tie up for a while to trade dried fish or charcoaled monkeys or other foods and crafts from their villages. They would buy soap and clothes and other city goods they needed, and then they would spend a few hours drinking in one of the bars before floating their way back home.

A couple of times, when the captain decided that too many of these boats were tied up, he sent his henchmen to cut them loose. Drunk men and women would go diving into the river after their boats from every direction, throwing their newly bought packages into the water or the nearest boat ahead of them. When the white tourists expressed their disapproval of these crackdowns by hissing and yelling at the machete-wielding policemen, the captain became angry and ordered a crackdown on us, too — confiscating the cameras of anyone caught taking pictures. The old rule in Zaire was that no pictures were allowed without various photo permits. That rule had been rescinded as part of an effort to encourage tourism, but not everyone knew or cared to know about the change. I had run into a few people in the bush who had asked to see my permits and had always been able to stonewall them. But on the boat, only one person's rules mattered and I was one of the few to escape the captain's injudiciousness. Those who had their cameras taken had to pay fifty dollars to get them back.

As the days went by, I became friends with a Dutch guy named Gerwin whom everyone called Kevin because it was easier to pronounce. He was a writer with a nihilistic bent, just out of graduate school and looking for some glimmer of hope in the world. He loved to talk about art and politics and religion. He was very upset about George Bush becoming president, and about the growing materialism in Holland, the decline of art in Europe, and the terrible living conditions in Africa. "This is still the Dark Continent," he said. "Very dark and very sad." We spent hours arguing about the nature of man, the direction of the world, the possibilities of progress. In the end, he pronounced me the first rational optimist he'd ever met and said that he would consider visiting America someday, after all, to see if it were really less bleak than Europe.

At night sometimes, after studying my new Lingala words for the day, I would lie on the deck looking at the stars for long hours before falling asleep. I kept the cover off my tent for the breeze, and it was a little hard to sleep with all the music and the people walking back and forth on adjacent passageways. The morning after picking up more people in Bumba, I discovered that someone had cut a small hole in my tent during the night and stolen my shaving kit. I was furious, not so much about the toiletries as about the hole in my beloved North Face tent.

I moved all my things from the two-story barge to the top of the newly added double-decker boat next to it. I set up my tent right in the middle of the curved roof so that there were no passageways nearby. I was all alone and no one could come up and bother my stuff without being clearly visible. I also had a better view. I meticulously sewed up the hole in my tent, and my place soon became the pilgrimage site for those tired of beer and backgammon and the increasing garbage down on the decks.

The one drawback was that it was so hot every afternoon that I could barely even walk across the roof and I became afraid the nylon on the bottom of my tent might melt. In the back, near first class, the pigs that were tied up in the sun would scream for hours — shrill, shrieking screams that started to make us all crazy after a while. Influenced by Gerwin's philosophies I began making myself embrace reality by not shying away from the unpleasant sights and offensive smells. We went together to see the aggrieved pigs one day, passing the tied up crocodiles and charred monkeys on the way. "They are just like us," Gerwin said as we watched the pigs panting and bellowing, trying to stretch their tethers into any patch of shade. In the middle of the next day I found some ants on a piece of bread I had been saving and almost ate them, just for the experience. And that night I stepped on something fleshy and hairy in the dark. Instead of just running on, I made myself turn on my flashlight to face my fear and look at whatever it was. It was a little boy asleep in the middle of the passageway. I just left him there and walked on.

I wonder what effect all of this is having on my mind, I thought later on that night. I wonder if I'm toughening up in a good way or if I'm possibly becoming too hardened and insensitive? I didn't really mind the rigorous travel, but the dirt and the heat and the chaos were definitely wearing on me, and I worried that I might be getting bent and tempered in some irrevocable way.

On the sixth evening storm clouds gathered in the sky and began showering us with huge raindrops. It had been so long since

I'd seen any rain that when it first started I sat out on the grass mat in front of my tent, letting the cool drops soak into me. When the storm intensified, I went inside my tent, stripped down and started reading while the storm blew outside. Soon, as the winds picked up, I found that I was stuck holding the corners down with my arms and legs spread out to keep the whole tent from blowing away. The poles bent so far that the tent's roof was almost flat on top of me. I watched through an opening as the rain crashed down on the wide river and I held my breath each time the lightning flashed, knowing I was not in a great spot if it hit the boat.

When things finally quieted down, I found that even with me and the gear inside, my tent had moved almost ten feet toward the edge of the roof. Down below, half of the tarps and stands and covers that people had rigged all over the boat had been blown away. Merchandise was scattered all over the deck and for the rest of the night people were crying and fighting and jockeying for new spaces with no help at all from the police. The two or three tourists who had moved their tents up to where I was moved back down, but I stayed, figuring a storm like that couldn't happen again.

By the end of the first week, tensions on the boat were high and the captain extended his tourist crackdown beyond camera violations. A British bond trader who was there on his honeymoon got arrested for drugs by the same police captain he had been smoking with the day before. He had to pay $300 to get the charges dropped and his beautiful, young French wife was so angry at him that she wouldn't make the payment for hours after he made the deal. Instead, she left him in the holding room and came and sat with me up on the roof.

She was fascinated that I was reading St. Augustine's *Confessions,* and seemed to be intrigued with the notion of confession in general. She told me that she was only twenty and that she had married her thirty-five-year-old husband because he reminded her of her father. "I have a very Freudian relationship with my father," she said matter-of-factly. She had read all of Freud's works in the lycée, and she thought that most people had an Oedipal complex of some sort. Hers was deep-rooted, though, she said, because her father was the most impressive man she had ever met. He was handsome and charming and very successful. Something in the bond trader had reminded her of him, so she married him. They were in the fourth month of a two-year, around-the-world honeymoon in their zebra-striped custom Land Rover and he was already disappointing her.

"I didn't know he was such a big mouth and a phony," she said. "I didn't know until recently that he even used drugs. We are just finding out all the bad things about each other because I am just starting to understand English. He doesn't even really speak French!"

I felt very sorry for her because in some ways she was like a child, and in some ways she already seemed very old. I wanted to tell her to leave him, to go home and get an annulment, to run away and come travel with me. But instead I told her that possibly for the rest of their lives, nothing would be as stressful and aggravating as the day-to-day travel in Africa. "Traveling like this is tough on anybody," I said. "Wait until you get to some fun places and if you still don't like him, then fly home and write it off as big adventure."

"It is certainly that," she said in her beautiful French/British accent.

After she bailed him out, he came up a few hours later to talk to me. She was napping in their cabin and I thought he was going to tell me off for interfering in his personal affairs, but in the British fashion, he just wanted to chat.

"Rather good setup you have here," he said, "nicely sited for the view." He asked me about my trip and told me that he envied me traveling alone, with no one else to worry about and deter me from my path. He said that even the Rover, which he had spent a year customizing, wasn't worth the hassle involved in getting past customs officials and crooked mechanics.

"I've paid almost as much in bribes as I paid for the renovations," he said. He explained to me that the top folded out into a sunny apartment that was "her space," and the bottom, a workshop with a small darkroom, a tool bench and a load of other things that seemed pretty useless for someone on the move, was considered "his space." I told him that it was all very impressive and that I particularly liked the zebra detailing.

"Well, you have to look the part," he said.

I wasn't sure what part he meant exactly, but I loved the thought of him pulling into a gas station in Arizona with that thing, or a campground in the Poconos. Chances are, though, he never got it out of Africa.

As we approached Kisangani, I passed the four-month mark of my trip. "Four down, four to go," I told Gerwin. I had been feeling a little homesick for a few days — I missed my family and my friends terribly, and I especially missed the comforts of my regular life. When I left, I had told everyone at home that I would be gone "eight months to two years," but I was beginning to feel like the shorter end would sit fine with me. I could see some of the negative effects that traveling had on people who were out too long, and I was starting to feel a little bit of what it was doing to me.

Like the Canadian guy, there were a few people on the boat who had been out on the road for a few years. Some of the Australians and New Zealanders were also basically living to travel. They would work long enough to save a bit of money and then go out and travel until it was gone and do it all over again. I liked the fact that they weren't living conventional lives, but the long-term folks all had a similar, agitated quality about them. They seemed as unsettled emotionally as they were physically, and rather than really exploring or even enjoying the places they went, they often seemed to be keeping a ledger: "This is my seventh major river," "This is my fifth continent." They were circling the globe almost on autopilot, picking up stories and experiences that they could only take to another place, because no one would really understand them back home. They were changed so much by their experiences that they couldn't fit in when they returned to their home countries. Though I loved traveling, I made a decision on the boat not to stay out so long that those kinds of negative changes would happen to me. I wanted to push myself far enough that I could grow and change for the better, but I didn't want to become so changed and so independent that I lost my ability to fit back into my life when I went home.

So I celebrated my minimal halfway point by toasting home with my friend Gerwin. I even ate most of the meat that came with my dinner that night and I soon regretted it. When the word went around that it might have been monkey, I had already been feeling a little sick. For the first time on the trip I had to take my antidiuretics and it was a long time before my stomach felt right again. Of course, when it rains it pours. The next day I discovered that the little white blister that had been growing on my foot was actually a bunch of worm eggs incubating. After I spent two hours cutting them out, I was walking around the boat wearing flip-flops and I slipped down the ladder between decks and cut the heel on my other foot all the way open. I traded with one of the locals for a pair of leather sandals that were less slippery and spent the next few days diligently trying to keep both cuts clean.

"At least the big cut made the first one seem less traumatic," Gerwin said, trying to be optimistic for a change.

Toward the end of the journey, the food and toilet situations had gone from bad to worse. The pigs had been moved inside on the lower deck right near the toilets and the kitchen. When the drains clogged up, the area became flooded and people had to wade through fetid, knee-deep water to get their meals (chest deep for the pigs). I couldn't even go down because of my cuts, but the women in the kitchen had taken a liking to me because I always tried to speak to them in Lingala. If no one was around to get my portion for me, I would hang my tin down from the second floor and they would fill it up for me. No meat.

I also used my developing language skills to employ a couple of kids to run errands for me. I would let them sit in my tent and look at my stuff, and buy them an occasional soda. One of them was terrifically nice and impressively bright. He rode the boat with his parents about three months out of the year, he told me. His dad ran one of the bars and his mother had a seamstress business going down below. The rest of the time he went to the missionary school in his home village east of Kisangani where he was headed again now. Someday, he said, he wanted to go study in Europe.

His buddy was not as impressive or as trustworthy. On the last day, when the boat was finally approaching Kisangani, I left him alone with my gear. I could see the buildings and the Kisangani rapids coming up ahead, and Gerwin and I didn't want to miss any of it. When the boat finally pulled into the docks just below the rapids, I discovered that my passport was missing. I could tell that a few things had been disturbed, but nothing else was gone.

When I told the police on shore what had happened, they gave me an official "safe passage" paper so that I could at least travel through to Bukavu and get my passport replaced. I didn't tell them that it was just a temporary passport and that I had another one with me also. The temporary one had all my African stamps in it, and some of the visas for East Africa. I went outside and watched the endless crowds of people coming and going from the boat with large piles on their heads, but I didn't see any sign of my two Zairian friends. My passport, with all the hard-won stamps and expensive visas, was gone.

INTO THE JUNGLE

ALL OF THE TOURISTS from the boat ended up at the same place in Kisangani, the gated Hotel Olympia that had converted its large courtyard into a campground. Everyone was glad to be off the crowded boat and there was a sense of accomplishment at having made it to the legendary Stanleyville. If any point can be considered the middle of Africa, Kisangani is it. Because of its position as the farthest navigable point on the Congo River, Kisangani has long been a symbol of the deepest penetration into Africa. Once you get there, there is no easy way out. You can take the river towards Kinshasa, one thousand miles away, or you can travel by land through deep jungles in every direction. Everyone in my group trying to get to eastern Africa, or even to southern Africa, was going the same way. The main road went four hundred miles east-northeast, coming out of the rainforest at the Ruwenzori Mountains near the border of Uganda.

Ironically, because Kisangani is such a remote outpost, it is one of the few towns in Zaire that has been fairly well developed. It was a commercial center for the Belgians before independence, and it has remained a trading and supply hub for all of the villages in the region. Everyday we were there, there was a huge public market in the town square and we walked among the stands buying vegetables for dinner and supplies for the road ahead. There is an airport, a movie theater, a few discos, and a few almost-European-style restaurants. But almost all of this existed in buildings that were old and falling apart. Though the infrastructure in Kisangani was better than any other place I'd seen in Zaire — with paved streets and modern utilities — as I walked around there was still a sense that it was all patched together, jury-rigged like the boats from Kinshasa, just enough to keep going for a bit longer.

Down by the river, at the Kisangani Falls, the old ways still prevailed. An intricate network of cone-shaped fishing baskets rigged on a series of beamed supports allowed fishermen and boys to climb out over the rapids and capture fish in the different rushing channels. Some would climb out every few hours to check their baskets, but others would sit out on the pylons while they waited for the fish, surrounded by the waterfalls, smoking their pipes, watching the sun set over the trees on the far bank.

Nearby was the riverfront palace that President Mobutu had built for himself, a gorgeous Palladian villa that looked like it was made of white marble. It was surrounded by a tall iron fence and to my surprise, there were no guards visible and the yard was half overgrown with weeds. Some teenagers who saw me looking in proudly told me that it was the "Maison du President." It was finished eight years before, they told me, and whenever he came to Kisangani, that is where he would stay. Their own houses were not far away, they said, pointing to a neighborhood of shacks nearby.

I asked if Mobutu came to visit often and they said that so far he had only been there twice, for a total of about ten days.

I asked them if they thought it was okay for their president to have so much money when so many people in the country were very poor and they just replied that yes, he was a very rich and very great man. "He has many houses," they said. "It is difficult for him to sleep in all of them." When I asked them how he got all of his money they seemed confused.

"He is a great man. He is very rich, with many houses and cars and many children," they said. "When he came to Kisangani, his boat covered the whole dock. He is the most powerful man in Africa."

"Well, he is one of the richest men in the world," I said, "but he has only worked in the military and as president. Before he was president, he had almost no money."

They had not known that he was one of the richest men in the world, but they seemed very pleased about that. I watched for a glimmer of awareness or resentment about the incongruity of his wealth, but there seemed to be none. They wished that he would come stay at his house more, but to them it seemed very natural for wealth and power to be tied up together so closely. I had the sense that a president who was not the wealthiest man in the country would seem as outrageous to them as Mobutu's corrupt government seemed to me.

I asked what else was good to see in town and the two boys took me to a factory that had fifteen Africans making jewelry and decorative carvings out of illegal ivory. It was run by a Belgian couple who welcomed me in to see if there was anything I might like. When I asked them if it was legal, they just shrugged. They hinted that the government was somehow involved in their operation. "By the time the ivory gets here," the man told me, "it has already passed through six or seven hands. If I don't buy it, somebody else will. It won't make any difference for the elephants." They didn't care about international law or about the ethics of what they were doing, just that there was a big market for their product. If there was any moral responsibility it rested on the people who bought the ivory. The only law they had to follow was the law of the jungle.

The second night in Kisangani I went out on the town with the tourist gang. Then late the next morning, after stuffing myself with pastries, I set out to go east across the jungle with the only other hitchhikers in the camp: Dave, the other American guy from the boat, and Jan, a jazz drummer from Denmark who was about my age. It seemed a little strange that with all the people and cars concentrated in the campground — more than I had seen together the whole trip — we couldn't finagle a ride from someone. But self-reliance is big in Africa and it felt good to be setting off into the unknown again. Even though the boat had been rough, it was comfortable and predictable in its own way. My only regret was that it hadn't worked out for me to travel a bit more with my friend Gerwin. I knew I would miss his conversation, and as we said our farewells that morning, we both said, "hope to see you soon," rather than "good-bye."

Jan and Dave and I hiked out to the police checkpoint on the eastern edge of town where all trucks had to stop for inspection. Everyone in the campground had been worrying so much about rushing to beat the heavy rains that we were all almost frantic. We figured we were the last or the second-to-last boatload of travelers who would make it through before three months of heavy rains would almost completely shut down the muddy roads, turning a four-day journey into four weeks or longer. I had read stories about trucks getting stuck so badly in deep mud holes that other drivers finally had to just fill dirt in around them and drive right over. Because the rains had already started a little, we figured there would also be a last-minute rush by transport trucks to get across, but that wasn't the case. We sat there all day without one truck leaving town.

I read a bit and when music from a nearby bar made it difficult to concentrate, I just sat back and watched the movements of the little town. Late in the afternoon I started feeling strange, and by six I could tell that I had a fever. When I went into my second cycle of chills, both Jan and Dave said, "You've got malaria." Jan had just gotten over malaria a couple of weeks before, and Dave's original traveling partner had been sent home from Ghana with it. Worse yet, there had been two tourists on the boat who were suffering from it and the mosquitoes had been pretty bad in Kisangani. I tried to remember the times that I had missed taking my daily antimalarial pills and how many times I had been bitten. I had tried to be careful, but obviously I had not been careful enough. About eight o'clock, I decided to take Fanzidar, a new malarial prophylaxis that had no resistant strains yet. As advised by the doctor in Paris, I had been saving it only in case I got sick, using older medications as my day-to-day precaution.

As I was taking a whole week's dosage as instructed, a truck pulled up heading our way. Though I had already set up my tent and was ready to crawl in for the night, I gathered my stuff together and climbed up top with the others. We set out into the jungle in the dark, and almost immediately the road was so bumpy that I felt like my fillings were going to drop out. I was feverish and dizzy and when I tried to sleep, my head would get jolted from side to side. By the time I realized that a megadose of Fanzidar might be kind of hard on my stomach, it was already too late.

Not far into the trip, the truck got a flat tire, and while they were fixing it, I walked a little ways down the dark road behind the truck, worried that I was going to get sick. My stomach heaved and shook a few times, but I kept myself from throwing up because I didn't want to lose the medicine I had just taken. When the truck broke down again a little while later I was feeling even worse and when I walked down the road, I had an attack of diarrhea. I climbed back up, feeling a little better and hoping that I could just settle down for the night, but I got attacks again and again and again, sharp cramps stabbing at my insides. Each time when I was just about to bang on the roof and say, "Stop the truck!" one of the tires would go out and they would stop in the middle of the dirt road and take it off and bang on it a bit while I ran out of sight.

By the fifth or sixth time, I was feeling dizzy and shaky and horribly wrung out. When I told Jan and Dave that I was getting worse, they were worried, but they were sure that when the medication kicked in I'd start to feel better. Though it was only about midnight, I felt an intense need to sleep. If I could just lie down for a bit in a stationary place, I'd be all right, I thought. Everyone else on top of the truck was sleeping as best they could while we bounced slowly along between the trees.

When we stopped the next time, the tire was in bad shape, and when I went down the road to squat down, I could see the big truck in silhouette and the men pounding on the tire with their wrenches. I woke up to the sound of the horn honking, probably twenty minutes later, and I could hear the driver revving the engine. I was lying in the middle of the road with my pants halfway down and I barely had the strength to pull them back up. It was so dark that I could hardly even see where the black trees gave way to the sky, and all I wanted to do was to find a spot to go to sleep. "Go on," I yelled, eyeing the ditch by the side of the road, thinking that I could crawl over there and sleep for a while and catch another truck in the morning. I didn't care about bugs or animals. I just didn't want to get run over. But then I woke up again to more incessant honking and I was still in the middle of the road and the truck was still fifty yards ahead, waiting for me.

I pulled myself up and got over to the truck. The driver said something to me angrily in Lingala and motioned for me to get back up top. My head was just up to the top rung when I passed out and fell ten feet to the road, landing with a big thump. I couldn't see straight when I opened my eyes, but I remember thinking, Ha! Now they'll know I'm sick. As my vision cleared a bit, I could see panic and concern in the driver's face. He touched the back of my head to see if I was bleeding, and I could feel the

bump already forming. Some of the other passengers woke up Jan
and Dave and I emphatically told them to leave me.

"I can't go any further in this truck," I said, "I just need to
sleep. I'll be fine."

"Just come to the next village," Jan said after speaking with
the driver. "He says its not far."

With their help I got back up on the truck and when I woke
up again, we were in a small village. Jan and Dave got our packs
down while I ran behind a tree. I got my sleeping bag out and
curled up in it with a sense of enormous relief. I was half surprised
that the others had stayed with me. I was glad that they had, but
I was especially surprised when I realized that the truck was staying too. "I'll be fine in a couple of hours," I said to Jan, "then we
can get moving."

"No worries," he said, "just take it easy for a bit." They insisted
that I drink some water, but it just kicked my stomach into action
again. Each time I went behind a tree, I felt better for a little
while. When they woke me up in the morning, it was still pretty
dark, but I had slept for nearly two hours straight and I was feeling much better. I told everyone I was good to go, but by the time
we were loaded up, I had already had two more bouts. When I got
a third attack and had to climb down, I told them to go on without me. They didn't want to leave me, but they didn't want to be
stuck waiting for me to get better either. When the driver said he
couldn't wait any longer, Dave announced that he was going to go
on and I was able to convince Jan to go on with him.

I went back to sleep for another couple of hours in the clearing where we had stopped and then woke up when I heard another
truck coming. By the time I got on my feet it had already gone by.
But the sun was up and I felt so much better that I crossed the road
to be in a good spot when the next one came. My stomach felt
more empty than it ever had and my clothes and sleeping bag were
covered with the red dirt of the village. Although I was a little
dizzy, I felt great compared to the night before.

Up and down the dirt road on both sides were little grass and bamboo huts. A few people were stirring here and there, but most of the village was still asleep. There were tall trees and dense jungle all around, but all the yards were cleared of vegetation and swept clean of everything but dirt, in the traditional Zaire fashion. I felt a little awkward just sitting out in their quiet neighborhood, but I didn't have much choice but to wait for another ride to come along.

I was planning to clean myself up a bit, but the effort of moving across the street made me exhausted again. I sat down on the ground, leaned against my pack and before I knew it, I was curled up on the ground, sleeping again. Dozing in and out, I heard the village waking up, and I could feel the sun clear the trees and get hotter and hotter on my face. I could hear children coming and going and I was thinking that there must be a schoolyard nearby when I felt a little hand poking at my shoulder. I woke up like Gulliver, surrounded by a crowd of wide-eyed kids, one of them leaning close. They all took a few steps back when I sat up and tried to speak. And they stayed clear when I shuffled across the road to go behind a tree. I could not even get completely out of their view and a few of them moved around anyway to get a better idea of what I was doing.

When I came back a couple of them seemed very worried. They tried to speak to me but I couldn't understand them.

"Je suis malade," I said to them, holding my stomach, then lying down to go to sleep again. "Je suis malade, c'est tout."

Some of them went off to school, but soon the crowd was back, and a tall, kind-faced man whom I took to be their teacher was shaking me awake. He could speak some French, and when I told him as best I could what had happened, he seemed very concerned. He told me that I should not travel and he and the kids helped me get my stuff to a shady spot in front of an abandoned hut a little ways down the road. It even had an outhouse in the back. We got my tent set up and he tried to get me to eat or drink something, but I wouldn't. I knew I was dehydrated, but I also knew I couldn't hold anything down and I figured getting my system active again would just make things worse.

They promised to come check on me and went back to school while I fell asleep, unable to keep my eyes open. I heard a couple of jeeps and trucks pass at different times, and at one point I heard one of them come back. It was Gerwin, and he was stunned when he saw me there.

"What happened?" he asked. I could see on his face that I looked pretty bad. When I explained it to him, he looked distraught. He started asking me about the foods I had with me and then he tried to insist that I drink some fluids. I wouldn't do it.

"You are dehydrated," he said. "You will have to replenish your salts soon or you will be in worse trouble." I was thinking that at least now I could get a ride with him and his friend Horst, a reticent German who owned the truck he was traveling in. But he wouldn't hear of it. He said he thought I should go back to Kisangani to the hospital, and that no matter what I shouldn't travel for a few days. I could tell that he felt awful about leaving, but Horst wouldn't wait for me to get better and if he hadn't wanted me in his truck healthy, he certainly didn't want me in there sick. Gerwin gave me a few packs of a powdered, Gatorade-like drink and told me to make some as soon as I felt able. Then he gave me a couple rolls of toilet paper and left. Horst waved disdainfully as they pulled off. I never saw Gerwin again, but he may have saved my life.

By midafternoon I started having trouble thinking straight and I was having trouble moving my arms and legs. It was like they weren't entirely connected to my body. I'd had to go back to the outhouse behind the empty hut a few times, but my stomach was feeling a little better. With the encouragement of the teacher, I mixed some of the powder with my water and drank a bit. It instantly made me feel better and though I wasn't able to hold it very long, my head cleared up a little and my joints felt reconnected. I kept making myself drink the solution, and in the evening I ate a little papaya and manioc paste that the teacher brought me. For a while I started feeling better, but during the night, in the middle of an awful rainstorm, things got bad again. My stomach and intestines lurched as the rain poured and poured, and I had to limp back and forth to the outhouse in the mud. Inside, water started dripping in, but by about three in the morning I was so exhausted from the ordeal that I just collapsed on top of my bag, mud and all, and fell asleep for the rest of the night.

When I woke up in the morning, I felt better, but I could tell that my system was still out of balance. I mixed more of the powder, and changed my clothes, putting the disgustingly filthy socks and shorts and underwear outside my tent. Before school, the teacher woke me up again and gave me some pineapple for breakfast with coffee, which he said was a medicament. By midmorning I felt so good that I read for a while and was thinking that I might even be able to travel on. At lunchtime, the teacher brought me more coffee and some papaya and bananas and manioc paste. The manioc paste would stop the diarrhea, he said, and the papayas and bananas would help me get better. Only later did I figure out that my electrolyte system was probably out of balance and that both were rich in potassium and glucose, just like the powdered solution I had been drinking.

One by one, most of the other tourists from the boat came by. They would stop and talk and wish me luck, and then give me some toilet paper before leaving. One guy whom I had talked to occasionally on the boat didn't even stop. He looked petrified that I might ask him for something. I could tell that the local kids thought it was very strange that no one gave me a ride, but they loved the point in the conversation when the toilet paper was handed over. After the fifth or sixth time it happened, they were waiting for the exchange and laughed when the roll was produced. I laughed too, feeling embarrassed but appreciating the absurdity of it.

By midafternoon I was feeling good enough that I decided to just keep heading east in small increments. I had no symptoms of malaria and I could tell that my stomach was getting more stable. I was even feeling a little hungry. I slowly packed my things, moving the stuff that was still damp into the sun and then packing it up when it dried. To my surprise, my down sleeping bag hadn't suffered much at all, but my tent was pretty dirty. I wiped them both down and hung them from tree branches, resting between each effort. I noticed that the dirty clothes I had left piled outside my tent were missing. I felt bad for anyone who was willing to steal them in that condition — I knew I was never going to be able to use them again. But then one of the students who had been particularly worried about me came walking up the hill from a nearby stream with the clothes thoroughly washed and neatly folded. They looked better than they had in a month. I was floored. I tried to give him some money, but he wouldn't take it and when I asked the teacher about it, he said, "It is not a problem. He sees that you need help and he is happy to help you."

While I was talking to the teacher, my bags all packed, ready to head on, a young Zairian man came biking along the road, heading east. When he saw me, he stopped abruptly and started speaking a mile a minute and gesturing in the direction he had come from. The teacher listened intently and then translated for me: the man had seen my picture on a passport in a village about twenty-five miles back toward Kisangani. Counting from Kisangani, we were at kilometer seventy-seven and the passport was in a village at kilometer thirty-seven, he said. The teacher asked me if this was possibly true and I told him about my passport being stolen. We were both amazed. A short time later an Austrian couple that I knew from the boat came by on motorcycles and said the same thing. "There is a boy waving your passport at the tourists who pass. He tried to sell it to us." I thought, well, I guess there is a reason for everything.

I moved my things back to the northern side of the road so that I could go back and get my passport. A Land Rover full of British tourists came along and offered me a ride before I even asked. They had been looking for me. "Everyone we see on the road tells us to take you to the hospital in Kisangani. I dare say you look a little better than we expected."

I thanked the teacher for doing so much to help me, and all of the kids for their concern and help as well. "Things would have been much worse for me if not for your help," I told the man. A small crowd waved good-bye as we pulled off. The village was gone from sight before thirty seconds had passed.

It was a little crowded in the Rover, but the four others didn't seem to mind. They were thrilled to be on their way back to Kisangani after running around for a few weeks in the jungle. They told me that the roads had already gotten pretty bad from the rains and they said that I would be crazy to try to go across by land rather than flying.

"You can take a flight from Kisangani to Goma for seventy dollars," they said. "If you go by road, it will take you weeks and cost God knows how much." Even in their comfortable truck, the roads were jarring me to pieces, making me feel weak and dizzy again. They were rushing because they wanted to get into Kisangani before dark. I didn't tell them about the passport until we were nearly at the village, and they weren't very pleased.

"Bloody hell, you've had a week!" one of them said. They told me they'd stop for five minutes and that I couldn't do anything that might cause problems with the authorities.

"I'll just pay the guy half of whatever he's asking and we'll be on our way," I said. But I lied. Even in my worn-out state, I couldn't stand the thought of paying someone for my own passport, especially if it was the kid from the boat.

When we pulled into town, children came running, and when I stepped out of the truck, it was as if royalty were in their midst. They all recognized me and a few of them ran off to get the older kid who had my passport. He was a cocky guy in his late teens, but when he saw me he got a little nervous. If there hadn't been such a crowd gathered, I think he would have run. Instead, after hesitating, he sauntered up with his jaw stuck out a little.

"Où est le passport?" I asked.

"Combien?" he asked, "How much?" I could see that he was holding it in his right hand, just behind his leg.

"Nothing," I said. "It's mine."

He started talking fast, saying that he had found it and saved it for me and that I should pay him or he would keep it. He wanted 15,000 zaires. When I didn't respond because I was trying to translate it into dollars, he got nervous and dropped the price. "5000 zaires," he said, about thirteen dollars.

I glanced at the British folks watching nervously from the truck and at the crowd of kids watching and some of the adults from the village standing around nearby. Under a tree I saw the boy from the boat who I thought had stolen it. When he saw me looking at him, he moved behind the tree.

"May I see it?" I asked. "Perhaps it is not my passport. Perhaps you do not have it."

The boy held up the passport for me to see and I snatched it out of his hand. It was mine alright.

I took two steps toward him. "This is the property of the United States of America," I said to him in English, trying to scare him. "See this," I said pointing to the seal inside and the warnings about theft or trade in passports, "You could get in big trouble for having this. Beaucoup d'problèmes. The U.S. Army would not be happy if they saw you with this. C'est mauvais. Mauvais pour moi. Très mauvais pour vous. Très mauvais."

He understood "U.S. Army" and he understood that I was angry. I think he might have thought that I was in the army. He lowered his price to a dollar and then just let the whole thing go, wanting to get out of there. I had the sense that he had been bragging about having the thing for a few days and the other kids couldn't figure out what was going on. As I turned to leave, the nice kid from the boat came running up with a plastic bookbag on. He was happy that I had come to get my passport back. But when I asked him if he had known anything about it, he started acting sheepish and said that the other kid had taken it and that he hadn't known how to find me. "You could have told the police," I said. He just shook his head, looking confused and upset.

When I got back in the truck the Brits were put out with me. They had seen everything. "You could have at least given him something," one of them said. "I mean, he did get it back to you." For the rest of the ride they ignored me, but I didn't really care because I was starting to feel worn down again. At least I had my passport back.

It was after dark when we got to Kisangani. I had them drop me off at the hotel where I had started from three days before. The Belgian woman at the desk was surprised to see me again. When I told her what had happened, she just shook her head.

Out in the courtyard, everyone was gone, except for a few people I didn't know. I set up my tent in a corner and went in to take a hot shower and shave. I looked in the mirror and barely recognized myself. My eyes were burning cobalt blue, sunken and shadowed by dark circles. My cheeks looked hollow and my ribs were showing more than I had seen in a long time. The cut on my foot from the worm eggs had closed up, but my heel was still cut open, suffering from the lack of attention the previous few days.

I tried not to think about the fact that everyone else was gone already, but I couldn't help feeling completely abandoned. The thought entered my head that I might have died if I hadn't had the salts, and that being so sick out there with no one to help me but strangers was the most horrible thing I had ever gone through. In the shower, I started sobbing uncontrollably, shaking as I leaned my head against the dirty tiles hoping the hot water would somehow cleanse me. Then I shaved, ate some crackers I had bought at the front desk, and went to bed.

STARTING OVER

WHEN I WOKE UP in my tent at the Olympia Hotel the next morning, I was famished. The sun was up and I felt a lot better than I had the night before. I drank some bottled water, ate a few crackers, got dressed, and set out into town to find some more food. The crackers seemed to sit pretty well, so I ordered some pastries and tea in a little café and pulled out my map to study my options. From Kisangani, there was another road that cut diagonally down to Bukavu in the southeast, where I was planning to go, but the middle 150 miles of it were just a white line — not yet completed. Running straight east and then northeast was the road I had already tried to take. Once it got out of the jungle, near the Ruwenzori Mountains, it was almost as far again straight south to Bukavu. I liked the idea of trying to go diagonally down the uncompleted route, but hiking those 150 miles alone was definitely a big question mark. It certainly wouldn't speed up my trip. When I had looked into the possibility before, everyone I had talked to had discouraged the idea.

"In a few more years, the new road will be fine," they had said, "but now it will be not only be slow, but the men working on the road will steal everything you have." The only one that I heard might be following that route was the Japanese guy, assuming he got his bike back.

"Screw it," I said to myself, feeling the weight of the world lift off my shoulders, "I'll just fly again." I had wanted to see the deep jungle, to see the Pygmies on their land and the monkeys and rare okapis at Epulu. But I figured the mountain gorillas near Goma and the jungle around there would do just fine. I was tired of worrying about the pace of my travel and being a slave to broken-down trucks and unpredictable weather. In my foggy, post-illness state, I had the notion that flying would free me of those kinds of hassles.

I bought an airplane ticket for $170 — only first class was available — and then I spent the rest of the day at the rundown airport waiting for the plane to come. It didn't show. After I went back into town to exchange my ticket for the next day's flight, I was so frustrated that I withdrew myself from the scene as completely as I could. I put on my Walkman and walked through the streets with my dark sunglasses on. I sat by the river with *Documentary History of the United States* — a book that I only took out in dire circumstances. I read Kennedy's inaugural address and Faulkner's Nobel Prize acceptance speech and a couple of others. Then after a dinner of canned beef-noodle soup, I went out for an ice cream and found a movie theater that was playing *Back to the Future.*

It was wonderful. For a few hours, I was far away, and when I came out of the theater, I stumbled upon a fast-paced women's basketball game with some very talented players. I watched for a while as they moved the ball up and down the court with accurate passes and graceful shooting from both outside and inside the lanes around the sagging baskets. There were some friendly locals cheering on the teams and they seemed pleased to have me there, watching my reactions to the game and asking me questions about my travels. By the end of the evening, I didn't feel quite so hemmed in.

On Sunday, when the plane didn't come again, I started to think that I had made a poor choice. The plane was being held up by bad weather, one person said. "Engine troubles," another told me later. When it was canceled late in the morning, I asked for a refund and got my things together to set out overland again. I bought a bunch of Band-aids for my foot, a store of food, and a few pints of bottled water. My stomach was feeling strong enough to have a big lunch, which I ate slowly, savoring every bite.

Late in the afternoon, I was back at the police checkpoint on the edge of town, starting over six days after I was there the first time. The sky was much grayer than it had been the last time. It had been raining most nights, and I knew the roads would be much worse already. But I had been feeling so much stronger each day, that I didn't really mind. Everything for the best, I thought. Chasing the plane just gave me a little time to get healthier. And this way I won't be running through the forest with a whole gang of other tourists. All for the best.

But whoever was making the plan decided that I needed more rest. For two more days I sat at the same spot, waiting for a ride and watching the world move around me. A young woman who had been badly beaten up came stumbling by, mumbling to herself. Another young woman fought with an older woman who appeared to be her drunk mother, trying to take a bottle away from her and getting knocked on the head several times for her effort. A guy came by in a Rustlers Steakhouse shirt. A woman who looked older than my grandmother came walking out of the forest nearby and headed down the road toward town with a heavy bundle of sticks on her back, held by a strap around her forehead. She shuffled along slowly as if she had been carrying them for thirty miles. Some British tourists I recognized from the Sahara came by and told me that another Rover was coming soon that could probably give me a ride, but none came. All the while, music blared from the nearby bar, shattering any sense of peacefulness the place might have had, and driving me crazy with its incessantly repetitive beats. And all day long, I watched the gendarmes shake people down and take bribes before letting them go about their business.

Fortunately they didn't bother me, but I could barely write in my notebook because I kept thinking up nasty things to say to them if they tried. Finally, late in the second day, the same teacher who had helped me when I got sick pulled up in a full truck. I hugged him. He was thrilled to see me too and he talked the driver into letting me ride with them. They were only going fifty kilometers, but I was glad to just get moving. When we went through the village where I had gotten my passport, I looked to see if I recognized anyone, but it was just a quiet, sleepy place. My guardian and his local friends let me off at dusk.

As I was looking around for a place to camp, a long empty tree transport truck came along. I flagged it down and the driver shrugged his shoulders and pointed to the back. There was no platform, just the narrow cross-braces for the logs. I had to sit on top of a strapped-down case of empty beer bottles and hold on tight. When he finally let me off at kilometer 122, I had round bruises on my rear end from the bottle tops, and I was completely covered with red dirt from the road.

I found a little hotel in the village, with mud walls and a thatched roof. It was pretty late when I got there and the family running the place seemed a little wary of me. When it started raining and I went outside in my gym shorts and showered in the warm, heavy rain, they were sure that I had lost my mind. Then, in the middle of the night, I woke up to find something wet and hairy moving in the palm of my hand. I yelled and threw it in the air, but it came back, flying into my face and hands as I screamed and swatted at it, inadvertently knocking it into my mouth. I gagged and yelped in horror, knocking it away. When I finally got the lantern lit, I could see something moving up in the corner — a small bat.

I shuddered and spit to get the taste out of my mouth, my heart racing wildly. I opened the door to get rid of the bat, and there in the
hallway was the whole African family, about as wide-eyed and pale
as they could get.

I tried to explain to them what had happened, but I didn't
know the word for bat. I waved my arms like a bat, but that didn't
seem to help matters. The youngest two kids started crying. No one
wanted to go in the room with me, but when I looked back in, the
bat was gone. I looked in every corner and then made myself look
under the bed too. It wasn't there. It hadn't gone out the door, so
my only guess was that it had flown out the open window, probably the same way it had come in.

For the rest of the night I didn't sleep very well, waking every
fifteen minutes until I finally just kept the lantern lit. In the
morning, I tried to explain to the family, but they didn't want any
explanations. When I left, they were very glad to see me go, rushing me out the door and quickly closing it behind me.

I set off on foot, not wanting to sit still. It was nice walking
down the narrow road through the jungle with the sun shining —
the first time I had been in really peaceful surroundings in a while.
I got a little worried when three trucks passed without stopping, but
an Office Des Routes dump truck, loaded with people including a
few Africans that I recognized from Kisangani, finally picked me up.
We stopped often to let people on or off, including a few small men
and women who were obviously Pygmies and usually got off in remote places rather than the villages. As we rode along, I occasionally saw a Pygmy in traditional dress walking along the road, a bow
in one hand and a quiver of arrows over his shoulder. But it was hard
to get a good look at them because they would slip off into the trees
as we went by and then come back onto the road only after we were
a few hundred yards past. One of the men riding with me said that
the Pygmy villages were all well off the road and difficult to find.
Though they wore pants and shirts when they went to Kisangani or
other towns along the road, they would take off those clothes as

soon as they got back into the trees. When I asked what they lived on, the man pointed to the jungle and said, "Everything needed to live grows there. The women find fruits and vegetables. The men hunt. But there is also gold and ivory and diamonds in the jungle, and now some try to live on these things."

All day we ran through mud puddles three- and four-feet deep, and twice we had to stop to pull other trucks out — the same ones that had passed by me earlier. At one point, the route was blocked by piles of gravel in the middle of the road. Each pile was so high that it blocked the view beyond it. Some trucks had tried to go around, but there was a big mud hole, so our driver went right up and over instead. On each side of the pile, I thought we might flip, but we didn't, and by the third pile, everyone in the truck was laughing and having fun, perhaps as much from the look of concern on my face as from the roller coaster motions.

In the town of Bafswende, where the dump truck let me off, there was no place to camp that I could see. I went into a small roadside café because I saw some Europeans in there, but when my eyes adjusted to the light the men seemed so menacing that I didn't speak to any of them. They looked like pirates and I could only guess that they were black marketeers, probably dealing gold and diamonds and ivory. One of them kept glaring at me. I could barely eat, worrying I might be in trouble somehow, if I didn't get out of there soon. I went outside as soon as I finished picking at my boiled chicken, and I was sitting by the side of the road waiting for another truck when a Land Rover came along, heading my direction. I stood up to flag it down, but before I could wave it came right toward me and stopped. The window rolled down and a pleasant looking blond-haired man said to me in English, "Hi, would you mind opening that gate for me?"

He was a missionary from Arkansas named Mike, and I had been sitting in front of the gate to his house. He invited me in and offered a room and a bath and a place at his table. I was covered in dirt again, so I gratefully accepted. He called his friend Bob on the walkie-talkie and the three of us had a festive dinner. They even had ice cream because Bob had just made a run to Bukavu in the plane. "Eat up," they said. "If we don't eat it, it'll melt by tomorrow."

I took a hot bath in a huge iron tub that looked like a horse trough and then we watched a video on a generator-powered VCR. The film was *The Emerald Forest*, a tale about a kid lost in the South American jungles. They seemed to be waiting for me to see some grand message in it, but I couldn't find any. It was just fun to watch a movie in the most remote place I'd ever been. It was a big time-out, capped by the fact that the guest bed, like all the others in the house, was a waterbed. Regular mattresses were too cumbersome to bring in by plane, they told me, so all the missionaries had waterbeds. I was so comfortable that I could barely sleep.

In the morning I had a leisurely breakfast with them and then went with Mike to see the church they had built. It was a big structure, open on all sides, with large, freshly hewn logs forming the supports. Nearby, the Linde River bubbled through some shallow rapids. He showed me where they would build a rectory next to the river, and where he and Bob hoped to put up new houses for some of the members of their parish. "First, they always want to build the pastor's house," he said, talking about African villagers in general. "That way they are assured that the church back home will keep sending money."

"Are they really that shrewd about it?" I asked.

"Oh, yeah," he said. "Half the village turns out for church on Sunday, but most of them just want the clothes and the food that we hand out occasionally. Even some of our best converts still practice all of their native rituals when they go home. If their child is sick, they don't pray or call us, they send for the witch doctor."

"But just getting them in the church is a step," he said. "The Lord can take it from there in His own way, I know. Sometimes, though, I wonder if this is all just a test for us. No missionary from our church has ever stayed more than a year."

I felt bad for him, trying to bend the whole village to his way of thinking. On the edge of town I had seen rows of little brick houses that some ambitious Belgian priests had built a long while back, obviously trying to civilize the natives in some way. But the natives liked their traditional huts better and the brick houses were now overgrown with weeds, occupied by only a few of the poorest folks in town.

One of Mike and Bob's parishioners was heading northeast along the road sometime before noon and they arranged a ride for me. I was able to ride up front for a change, but the roads were in bad shape and the truck was barely up to it. We had to go slowly most of the way, rocking and creaking our way around and through mud holes. There were a couple of places where there were trucks stuck dead at big holes. If the lead truck was stuck, everyone would help dig it out and cut channels to drain the water away. When that truck finally got through, it would wait for the next one to go into the hole and it would help pull it out before moving on. The rule of the mud holes was, don't drive off until the guy behind you is on dry ground.

In midafternoon we reached a line of trucks waiting at a very deep hole. We waited two hours without moving before I finally thanked the driver and set off on foot. Up at the hole, there were thirty men engaged in what was turning into a major construction job. A soldier who had been riding on one of the trucks was trying to lead the effort, but everyone was pretty much just yelling at each other and doing their own thing. I walked on down the road, past a line of trucks waiting in the other direction. Pretty soon I was alone again, walking down the green corridor that was cut through the trees by the narrow dirt road. I figured I'd just keep walking until some of the trucks started coming by. I was just forty kilometers from Nia Nia, where the road split, and I knew that once I got there, there would be additional eastbound vehicles coming down from the towns up north.

I walked through one very small village, scaring the heck out of a few of the locals as I came out of the forest, especially some kids who had apparently been told the widespread childhood tale about white people eating little African children. There was nothing in the village but huts, so I just kept walking. As the sun started to set, I got a little worried about where I would sleep. My pack felt very heavy on my shoulders, pulling and pinching everywhere so that I cursed the manufacturer and the guy who sold it to me. I had covered about seven miles when it started getting dark. The trees around me seemed to close in a little, and the jungle came alive with noises. Everything was so overgrown that I couldn't see anyplace suitable for camping. But just when I was starting to get a little scared, I came around a bend and saw a footbridge over a stream next to the road.

The road turned up a hill and a good number of huts appeared on either side. Again I sent a few kids scurrying in the darkness. It turned out to be a sizable village and I was thrilled when I found a little café open for business. I had chicken with rice and a couple of bottles of beer for dinner. The owner sent word to the only European in town that I was there, and he came down and ate with me. He had greasy hair, a triple chin, a huge stomach, and was a gold and ivory dealer who had lived in the area for a long time. He told me stories of going hunting with the Pygmies and of getting taken to gold mines deep in the forest that he had no way of finding again. The local people would bring him anything he asked for, he said, and some things he didn't even want. He had stopped trading in gorilla and monkey products years ago, but they would still bring them to him whenever they could. A black leopard skin had even come in a few months before and he had to buy it just for himself because he knew that it might attract trouble to trade it — unless the right buyer just happened to come along, of course. I didn't even ask to see it.

He also talked a lot about politics and told me that twenty years before, the road I was on was easy to travel, even at this time

of year. "Mobutu purposely keeps the roads in this region bad because there have been rebel uprisings in the past and if another
one happens, he wants it to be difficult for them to move," he said.
"Every year the roads get worse and the government refuses to fix
them." He said that Zaire was one of the richest countries in the
world in terms of resources, but that Mobutu had systematically
taken for himself every bit of public wealth that he could get his
hands on. He told me that Mobutu's hometown of Gbadolite, near
the northern border, was just a tiny jungle village, but that it now
had a runway big enough to land a 727 on and four miles of paved
roads so that Mobutu's son could drive his Maserati around.

When it got late, he said good-bye and wished me luck before
staggering out of the place. The owner moved the tables so that I
could sleep on the floor. I slept restlessly all night and left at six-
thirty the next morning, not wanting to miss any trucks that
might be going through.

But no trucks passed all day. So I just kept walking through
the forest toward Nia Nia. I passed through a number of little
towns, and stopped only for lunch with some old men under their
traditional town pavilion, and then again later to listen to beautiful singing coming from an afternoon church service. Flowers were
blooming in front of the church and the sun was out and there was
no missionary leading the service, just the local people intensely
celebrating God in their own way. I was so captivated by the scene
that I took out my camera to take a couple of pictures, but when
I did, some kids saw me and came running out to get in the shot.
Pretty soon the whole church was empty. The singing stopped and
everyone spilled outside to get a look at me and get in my photo.
I was so embarrassed that I took two shots as quickly as I could,
thanked them and headed off down the road.

Before I was out of town, some young men asked to see my
photo permit. When I told them that I didn't have one and that
they weren't required anymore, they said I was wrong. They were
now required again and I would have to pay them a fee or give

them my film. I tried to laugh and play it off, as I had learned to do, but this was Zaire, not Mali. When they kept getting more belligerent, I finally told them to check with the police in town and I kept walking. They talked among themselves, obviously angry, and then started following me along the road. When I realized that I had maneuvered things so that I had not only made them angry, but was now alone on the road with them, I started to get a little worried. Two of them left the road and started moving through the trees on either side of me, while the third just walked further behind down the road. I tried to stay calm and keep the panic from rising while I considered my options. And then I didn't hear anything for a while and they were gone.

I walked into Nia Nia with blistered feet, feeling pretty pleased with myself. I had walked fifty kilometers through the forest and no truck had ever come past. I felt like I had been traveling fresh ground rather than a well-traveled tourist path. And Nia Nia just added to the feeling. It was a wild place with a frontier feel. There were people making deals for diamonds and gold and food and gasoline in every little shop, in the clapboard cafés, even out in the middle of the muddy street. The action was so frenetic that I nearly bought a big diamond myself for one hundred dollars, until I realized that I didn't even know if it was real, let alone what quality it was. I settled in at a table on the porch of a rustic little restaurant and ordered a bowl of manioc root *fufu*, with a piece of unknown meat on top of it. I ate it slowly and watched the road and read. I had eaten the *fufu* a few times before, but this was the first time that it really tasted good. I'm not sure if I had finally acquired the taste, or if the long walk had affected me. I wasn't going to eat much of the meat, but my body was craving the protein and it tasted so good too that I ended up eating the whole thing and had to keep myself from ordering another bowl.

Despite all the action in town and the additional road coming in from the north, for a long while I didn't see any trucks or jeeps heading my way. After I finished eating, I leaned my pack up against a fence outside the restaurant and took a nap for a while. Around sunset, a couple of trucks came limping into town from the north, kicking up dust like a pair of stagecoaches. They told me they had an open spot to Epulu, a village built around the cap-ture station for the endangered okapis, that was on my list of stop-ping points anyway.

Epulu was just another seventy-five miles to the east, but the road from Nia Nia was so bad, and the trucks were so worn out, that we only covered fifteen miles before stopping at 1:00 AM to sleep for the night. Everyone spread out blankets on the ground, but it started raining as soon as we got to sleep, so we all squeezed in under the trucks. Before it even got light, the driver started the truck with all of us still under it, scaring the hell out of everyone and starting our day with a good blast of exhaust. It was the first of many. For the rest of the day the trucks went so slow that half the time the exhaust was billowing around our heads, the other half we were dodging tree branches and holding on for dear life as we plunged through colossal mud puddles. Along the way, people who were walking down the road sometimes passed us two or three times before we finally got up enough speed to get beyond them. It was the slowest travel of my trip.

By the time we pulled into Epulu late in the afternoon, I was pretty tired, but I was rewarded with a beautiful camping place next to a clean, rushing river. As soon as I got my tent set up, I stripped down and took a bath in the river. It was cold enough to really cool me off and just warm enough that I could stay in for a while. Afterward I felt totally refreshed and it was difficult to put my dirty clothes back on. I found the cleanest things I had and then washed the others in the river and laid them on the shore to dry.

Before dinner I went to check out the okapis, rare little ani-mals that look like a cross between zebras and llamas. The village was founded at the place where the first okapi was captured by Western scientists early in the twentieth century, and it was still functioning primarily as a research station and preserve. There were pens where sick okapis were cared for and where others were kept for breeding. I struck up a conversation with a couple of the scientists who were doing research that was sponsored by the New York Geographical Society and they invited me to join them for dinner. The British couple that I had seen in Kisangani drove in also, and we all ate together in the village café.

The scientists told us that their biggest challenge was convincing the Pygmies not to hunt or capture the okapis. They had been able to establish a big reserve for the animals in the surrounding jungles, but the Pygmies hunted everywhere, and there was no way to contact a lot of them. They told us stories of going on long trips into the jungle to count or trap the okapis, and running into hunting parties of Pygmies who would appear all around them before they ever heard anything.

I slept deeply that night, dreaming about the mysterious little animals and their mysterious human counterparts. In the morning I wanted to stay on at Epulu, but the roads were dry and it looked like more rain was coming, so I hopped on the first truck that came through around 10:00 AM. It was almost as slow as the truck the day before, but five times more expensive. The driver insisted that I ride up front with him, his two assistants, and a big leg of smoked meat with the hair and tail still on it. He was a surly Ugandan who said he hated coming into Zaire, except for the women. He could speak English, and he kept asking me if I liked the prostitutes in Zaire. He was emphatic that I should go to Kenya via Uganda rather than Tanzania. "The people in Rwanda and Burundi and Tanzania are savages," he said. "They are backward countries." In Uganda, he told me, there were discos and good roads and hotels with television, cheap prostitutes and plenty of drugs. I liked the part about the good roads, but to go to Kampala he wanted to charge me nearly a hundred dollars, and I had heard worse things about the Ugandan police than any others in Africa. Most of all, I really wanted to see the mountain gorillas in Rwanda or near Goma on the eastern border, even if the people were "savages."

As we drove along, every time the driver saw a charcoaled monkey for sale on the side of the road, he had to stop and check the price. We would wait for the Pygmy who had placed it there, spiked on the end of a spear, to come out of the jungle and then he would debate with the guy for fifteen or twenty minutes over the price. The monkeys usually looked like they had simply been tossed onto a fire and cooked until they were burnt to a crisp. And the way they were singed during this process, the bodies looked pretty normal, but the faces looked like they were screaming — the mouth wide open and the teeth showing all the way back. By the end of the first day, we had two charcoaled monkeys in the cab and nearly a dozen stowed up top, making it hard for the other passengers to find a safe place to sit.

When we stopped for the night, the driver and his assistants cooked up a pot of *fufu* with some of the monkey, which I respectfully declined. But the next evening, after fourteen hours of practically nonstop driving to go just fifty miles, I was so hungry that I ate a piece of the hairy goat leg that had been resting behind the seat. By the time I smelled it cooking, I might have even considered the monkey.

On March 21, the slow Ugandan truck finally broke out of the jungle, opening up distant vistas for the first time in a month. For weeks the horizon had been defined by trees that loomed nearby, or at best, by a bend in the river. But just east of the town of Mambasa, the landscape started getting hilly and the forest opened up to reveal the great brown and green Ruwenzori Mountains. The thick forest ended so abruptly that I found myself leaning out the window to watch the tree line recede. I was somewhat sad to see the jungle go, but I was ecstatic at having made it across and I had to fight back urges to get out and start jogging on ahead of the slow-moving truck, or to just to set up my tent on one of the rises and stay there for a while, looking at the mountains on one side, the jungle on the other, and the rolling green valley in between. As I leaned out the window of the truck, I savored a sense of growing satisfaction as I realized that I had made it across, I was almost in East Africa.

At Komanda, my truck turned south and limped along the western side of the Ruwenzoris, driving all night to go seventy miles to Beni and then another eight tortuous hours to go thirty miles to Butembo. I had been told that the roads would be better once we started heading south, but on the first stretch at least, they were not. By the time I got to Butembo late in the afternoon, I was thoroughly exhausted, but heartened by the progress. I was planning to rest there a bit, but the town had such a dreary combination of sullen people and threadbare cinder block buildings that I put on my pack and hiked straight to the southern edge of town to wait for another ride.

SANCTUARY

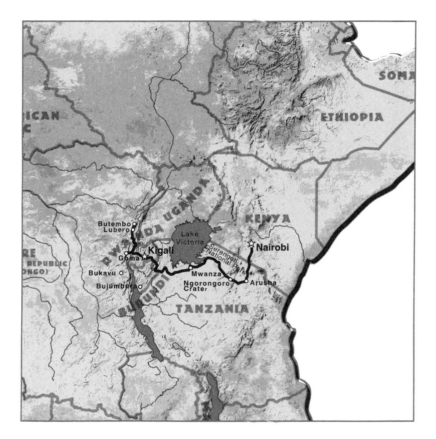

I had seen a herd of elephant traveling through dense native forest . . . pacing along as if they had an appointment at the end of the world."
ISAK DINESEN

ACROSS THE EQUATOR

I WAS PICKED UP OUTSIDE of Butembo by a taciturn, fast-driving Frenchman who took me a little further south to Lubero. It was just thirty miles from Butembo, but by the time I got there, I felt like I was in another country. When we crossed the equator halfway through the drive, I told the man that it was my first time across, and he just grunted. I'm not sure what I wanted him to do, but stopping for a picture might have been nice. To my surprise, we started winding up and down through lush, hilly farm country that looked to me more like China than Africa. The air got chilly and foggy. I could smell dung fires burning and the people had thick, thatched roofs on their houses and cows and chickens in their yards. In Lubero, I got a room at a comfortable little hotel and had all kinds of grilled vegetables for dinner — tomatoes, onions, peppers — and then fresh fruit for dessert with a cup of hot milk that they called tea.

I thought the Frenchman had dropped me in a unique town, but in the morning, after a breakfast of hot milk with bread, I caught a bus going further south and realized that I had transitioned to an entirely new region. It felt like a different continent. It was pouring rain in the morning and I had to put on my long underwear and my fleece-lined jacket to stay warm. Even when the rain stopped it was wet and chilly and the low clouds hung on the sharp edges of the green hills as if they'd been caught trying to slip over. All morning the road wound up and down and around steep hills that were dotted with farming villages and friendly people. At each place we stopped there were people selling whole grilled onions, boiled peanuts, and even roasted corn-on-the-cob. The first time I saw the corn I was so surprised that I didn't even buy one. But when I got one at the next stop it tasted so wonderful that I bought two more. Only the jealous stares of my fellow passengers kept me from buying a dozen.

After noon, we crossed a seven-thousand-foot pass and then made a long descent down the Kabasha Escarpment to the parkland around Lake Idi Edward. The lake and most of the plain were literally glimmering below us from all of the water. I almost fell out of the window straining to see if there were animals down there. Every bush looked like a wildebeest to me and every tree an elephant. On the long trip up the river and across the jungle, I had almost forgotten about the possibility of seeing animals on the plains in East Africa. It would be the fulfillment of a dream that had been with me for a long time.

For two hours, the bus drove through the park, passing gazelles and antelope, baboons and wild boars, hippos, and a small herd of wildebeest. Strangely, the scenery soon became more exciting than the animals. I was captivated by the long horizons of the wide, flat plain with its mountain backdrop. Big clouds hung low over everything, making the landscape even flatter and wider. At times on the narrow, viewless roads of the jungle I had felt a little claustrophobic, but it was not until I got back to the vast, open space that I realized how starved my senses had been. With the wide vistas and the deep greenery, it was a combination of the best of the desert and the jungle. It felt like a great aesthetic reward after months of deprivation, made all the more so since I had not expected it there, on the Zaire side of the border.

But just in case I had any doubt about where I was, the roads south of the park turned horrible again. During the last few hours into Goma the bus bounced and shook so badly that I could barely see straight by the time we got there. It began raining again and because I had heard horror stories about thieves at the campground in Goma, I took a clean room at the Protestant mission and didn't come out until the following evening. I cooked a dinner of rice and vegetables, took a long shower and started a new book before falling into a deep, deep sleep. In the morning I got out my map and looked at the green spaces I had covered over the past month and at all of the solid red lines (for paved roads) between Goma and Nairobi. I could be there in three days if I wanted to. I had definitely made it across.

In the evening I went out to the Au Rendez-vous Restaurant, where other travelers and some local Peace Corps volunteers were hanging out. I drank a few beers to celebrate and found out what I could about the best routes and sight-seeing opportunities from there. To my surprise, I recognized only a few of the travelers. My crowd from the boat had already dispersed and most of the tourists were people who were just traveling around in the east. I had planned to go to Rwanda to see the mountain gorillas, but everyone said it was a better trip on the Zaire side and less expensive. Visiting the lowland gorillas near Bukavu was like going to a zoo, someone told me, but Jane Goodall's chimpanzee reserve on Lake Tanganyika was really worth the effort if you could get there. The problem was that it was necessary to go into Burundi and catch the boat down the lake to her Tanzanian camp because it was too difficult to get there by road within Tanzania. After listening to as many stories as I could, I decided to go see the gorillas in Zaire and then cross into Rwanda and work on my Burundi visa from there. If I felt like it, I figured I might even go see the gorillas at Diane Fossey's old camp in Rwanda as well.

I got my visa for Rwanda and went to a special tourist office to pay one hundred dollars to book a visit to the gorillas. They would only take American dollars — in cash, which I didn't have. I had to run all over town trying to get someone to cash my traveler's checks. After near misses with a number of French merchants, I found a local African optometrist who was willing to do it without even charging a commission. It felt strange to be seeking monetary help from an African after having the roles consistently reversed for so long, and it felt even stranger to be handing over so much money to the tourist office when I had gotten used to spending just three or four dollars a day. When I first heard the fee, I wasn't going to go, but then I remembered that it might be a little while before I made my way to Goma again.

GORILLA HIGHLANDS

I SET OUT FROM GOMA to see the mountain gorillas on Good Friday. It was raining again when I left town. The rainy season had definitely arrived and I could only imagine what the muddy roads I had traveled the previous weeks looked like now. Heading back north and then east towards the border, there were numerous steep volcanic hills, many of them rising right up out of the flat farmland like jagged teeth. Everything was either dark green or dark brown, the rich volcanic soil showing through even in the places where the crops were full grown. The gorilla reserve was in the biggest of the mountains up in the Virunga National Park, tucked in a border zone where Zaire, Rwanda, and Uganda all come together.

I was dropped off in a village near the main road and spent a few hours hiking on a gradual incline, just to get to the base of the mountain. Then I began a long hike up to the lodge. The views on the way up were terrific, but it was much farther than I had expected. When I finally saw the lodge appear, I was so grateful that I laid down in the grass to let the sweat dry a bit before making the final assault. My clothes were already wet from the rain, and with the humidity, nothing was drying quickly.

When I got up to start walking again, a man was coming down from the lodge to meet me. He was blond and Caucasian, and he gave a big wave when he saw me standing. I couldn't imagine what he might want and we both walked another ten minutes before finally reaching each other. He welcomed me and deferentially introduced himself as the manager of the lodge. He wanted to carry my backpack, but I wouldn't let him, so he took my day pack instead. We made small talk as we trudged up the hill and were nearly to the beautiful glass and wood lodge, perched right on the ridge, when we realized that he had mistaken me for a different customer. His demeanor quickly changed.

"I'm terribly sorry, you're not in our lodge at all," he said, somewhat annoyed. "You would be in the cabin over there." He pointed to a big, rustic log cabin that was another two-thirds of a mile up the ridgeline.

"Well, thanks for carrying the bag," I said to him while eyeballing the white-coated, white-gloved African attendants who were staring at me.

"How much is your place anyway?" I asked, thinking his lodge looked so nice that I might splurge for a fifteen- or twenty-dollar room. He gave me a price list that showed rooms starting at $375, meals included. The lodge was owned and run by the famous safari resort TreeTops, and the brochure indicated it had been open just three months.

"Thanks, I'll give it some thought," I said, pulling my pack back on and heading off to the cabin. I passed the rangers' station, the small visitors' center, and after fifteen minutes got to the big log cabin. It was a classic park cabin with a central kitchen and a bunk room on each side, one for men and one for women. I was the only one there. Signs said that it was built and maintained by the Frankfurt Zoological Society. There was firewood stashed neatly next to the stove, jugs of fresh water, and utensils for cooking and eating. The front porch looked out onto the valley that I had come from, gray clouds, green volcanic mountains, checkerboard farm fields all down below. And it was quiet — so quiet that I didn't quite know what to do with myself. I could feel the temperature dropping, so I got a fire going in the stove and changed into dry, warm clothes and then sat out on the porch for an hour and a half thinking and watching the sun set. It felt almost tragic to be there all alone, and at the same time I felt like the luckiest person in the world.

I listened for gorilla noises, but I didn't hear any, even though the thick forest started just behind the cabin. I could see a good bit of their habitat because there was a high peak nearby that marked the place where the three borders met, with acres and acres of trees leading all the way up to it. In various patches of that forest, I knew that there were families of gorillas moving through the trees, eating, mating, fighting, bedding down for the night. As I sat on the porch, watching the stars and listening to the night, I remembered my great-great-uncle who had spent months exploring and tracking gorillas in the same region seventy years ago. He had gone home with journals full of scientific observations, hundreds of animal skins, and three small mountain gorillas — the first ever brought to Europe and America in captivity. I wondered what he had thought when he camped in these mountains. Had he seen the same skies outside his safari tent? Had he heard the same noises in the night? Had he felt the same nervous excitement?

At six-thirty in the morning, after lying awake much of the night, I got up to stoke the fire and watch the sun rise. It had gotten very cold during the night and I quickly boiled some water to make a hot cup of tea. At 7:15, I saw a few of the rangers gathering at the station and I went down to talk to them. I had been given some materials that explained the gorilla visits, but it had been so quiet on the hilltop that I wasn't even sure we'd be going.

From far away these Zairian men looked sharply dressed in their khaki uniforms, but up close, they were a scraggly bunch. They told me that there were only two other tourists at the TreeTops lodge, and that if those tourists chose to take an afternoon visit, I would be going alone with the rangers in the morning. It was the beginning of the off-season, they told me, and they were scheduled to stop the tours for a three-month break in another week and a half.

I went back to the cabin and had a piece of bread and more tea for breakfast, got dressed for the day, and then went to the small visitors' center to look at some of the pictures until it was time to go. There was a history of the gorilla visits and some information on how to interact with them. The gorillas moved in families of about thirty to forty, it said, with one silverback as the leader, ten to twenty "mamas," and usually ten to fifteen youngsters at one time. When the male children got old enough, they would go off on their own until they were strong enough to challenge another silverback for the control of a family. The traditional image of the mountain gorilla beating its chest was primarily a product of those male to male encounters, the exhibit said, but it was also a part of the gorilla's whole system of avoiding conflict through intimidation.

The gorillas that lived in the mountains nearby had been slowly habituated to the presence of humans. They now tolerated humans as they would other animals in the forest, but if we got inside their space, the females would react first by growling and charging. If the silverback thought that there was any real threat to his group, then the consequences could be more serious. He would first show his anger with thunderous roars and chest pounding, then warning charges, and finally real fighting charges. Most of the females were about four-and-a-half feet tall and weighed nearly six hundred pounds, the literature said, while the silver-

backs were typically about a foot taller and weighed over one thousand pounds, with chests even wider around than they were tall. If
one charged, the park commission advised, you should tuck up in
a ball and let them bat you around a few times. If you didn't run or
fight back, they would almost never harm you.

When I went outside, the guards, who were armed with rifles
and machetes, reiterated the last part. "If they charge, just cover
your head and stay still," they said. I was disappointed to see that
the couple from the lodge had decided to come along. They were
in their fifties and looked like they had just stepped out of an
Abercrombie and Fitch catalog. They were so clean and well-
pressed that at first I had trouble concentrating on what they were
saying. I hadn't seen anyone who looked so well-groomed since I'd
left Europe. I wondered what they thought of me, with my worn
jeans, my well-weathered blue T-shirt, and the windbreaker that
I'd been laundering in muddy water for three months. They
seemed a little disappointed that I was there, but mostly they were
just nervous about the gorillas, especially the woman, who almost
lost her nerve after the rangers went through the warnings.

At about 8:30, we all hiked into the forest on a path that
started right behind my cabin. There were three of the local
rangers with us, two in front and one in back. The lead guide was
the tracker. It was his job to find where one of the nearby gorilla
families had slept the night before, and then follow their tracks
to where they were feeding that morning. In this way, the
rangers charted the movements and made a head count of three
or four different families each day. By coordinating with similar
programs in Rwanda and Uganda, and by moving quickly against
poachers over the past seven years, they had stabilized the
rapidly declining gorilla population in that preserve at about 200
— half of the wild population in the world. There were some in-
dications that the population was starting to increase again,
though inbreeding had become almost as big a problem as
poaching.

We walked quietly through the thick woods for over an hour before we found nests from the night before. Each was a pile of recently broken branches and leaves with a round depression from their weight and a small brown piece of gorilla spoor in the middle. In the thick forest, the gorillas had stripped enough leaves off the plants around their sleeping area that some sunlight was allowed to get in. As we stood there illuminated by shafts of light, my heart started beating faster knowing that the large animals had been there just a few hours before and that they were undoubtedly nearby. The wealthy couple stood almost back to back, their eyes wide as they searched the forest in every direction.

The head guide picked a piece of the gorilla dung out of one of the larger nests, squeezed it a little and then held it up under his nose. He studied nearby branches, checking to see how they were broken, and then motioned for us to follow deeper into the forest. "Same, every day," one of the rangers whispered to me as he pointed to the nests, meaning that the gorillas would defecate in their nests before heading out for the day. "Warm is nearby," he said. "Cold is not near."

"Why does he smell it?" I asked. The ranger thought about this and shrugged.

Every few hundred yards we would stop and listen for a moment, and the tracker would inspect the ground and the trees for signs. He was so theatrical about it that I started to think he was just kidding around. But one time when we stopped he held his hand up for us to be quiet and we could hear some branches breaking nearby. I didn't see anything initially, but when I looked toward one of the noises, I could see a big patch of black in with the green, then another and another. We took a few steps forward and soon branches were crackling all around us. There were gorillas everywhere, even little ones in the trees above.

My impulse was to back right out of there, but the gorillas' countenance was so gentle that they soon put me at ease. When we moved slowly around to get a better look at some of them, they just watched us shyly and continued eating their leaves. The big silverback looked twice the size of the others. He stayed a short distance apart, wreaking havoc on a big patch of stalks, eating as much as he could lazily fit in his mouth. He ignored us for the most part, keeping his back to us and grunting occasionally if we moved near his space.

In his pack, he had twenty-three "mamas," seven babies, and a few young males who were already starting to show a little silver, but were not yet big enough to be kicked out of the clan. The biggest of the babies ran up and down the trees and stalks, wrestling with each other and annoying the older gorillas. Two of them climbed out on some of the high stalks, going farther and farther until the stalks broke, dropping them right on top of some of the feeding mothers. They were sent tumbling with a quick swat and a growl, and then they went looking for some other stalks and did it again.

The smallest babies were more sedate, little fur balls just learning to crawl and climb. The littlest one became curious about us and crawled right over to me to take a closer look. I squatted down with my arms resting on my knees and he reached out to touch my forearm, running his little leathery finger back and forth on my bare skin. He was so irresistibly cute that I wanted to pick him up. But the mama who appeared to be the babysitter started growling and one of the rangers asked me to move aside as he carefully pushed the baby away with the butt of his rifle. This made the mama more angry and she charged right at me, moving like lightning and baring her sharp teeth. I took a step back and ducked my head. But she had pulled up a few feet away and sauntered off into the jungle, following the silverback who had decided to move to another spot. I was a little embarrassed that I had jumped back when the rangers had been so emphatic about not running from the gorillas, but when I looked up, the guard who had been next to me was five feet back and the rest of the party was ten feet behind him.

We stayed with them for an hour, following them each time they moved to a new feeding site. The guards said that they thought the baby had touched me because I was wearing a short-sleeve shirt and he had never seen such white skin. I put my jacket on and we tried to stay a little further back, but the same mother charged me again, this time swiping her hand so close to my head that I felt my hair move. I was squatting down this time and I just turned my head and shoulders away. By the time I glanced up, she was already twenty feet away.

But by then I found I wasn't really frightened. They were so obviously gentle and so aware of their surroundings that I felt to-tally trusting of them. "No one who looks into a gorilla's eyes — intelligent, gentle, vulnerable — can remain unchanged . . ." the naturalist George Schaller once wrote, and I understood what he meant. They looked like they might start speaking if you stayed long enough. But I could also tell that after a while we were being intrusive and bothersome by constantly following them. Finally the silverback went into an area of thick brush where we couldn't follow, and he growled a few times as if to say, "Okay, the session's over. Get out of here." A few of the mamas had to cross by us to follow him, and the babysitter who had feint-charged twice de-cided to just sit on the path in front of us. We waited for a little while, but then she sat back defiantly and started eating a nearby shrub. The head guide decided to scare her away by dropping a thin tree near her. It was a good plan except that the tree was taller than he thought and the branches fell right on top of her. This time when she charged she really was mad, but she still didn't do anything except scare the heck out of the ranger.

We left reluctantly, looking back often as we walked in silence through the depths of green leaves and yellow light. When we stepped back out of the forest, it was like stepping out of a dream. We had to walk another mile to get back to the cabin, the sun just starting to bake the dew off the long grass near the edge of the woods, causing steam to rise up around us.

The couple was so thrilled that they could barely speak. I gave them a quick tour of the cabin before they headed down to their lodge and I could tell that they almost would have preferred my place. "Come up for tea later if you like," I said.

"Come down for a drink," they replied. We waved as they headed down the path toward their lodge. The British manager came out to greet them, practically running up the path.

I took the last of my bread and a can of sardines down to the rangers' hut and ate at the picnic table with the guides. They told me about their work and said it would actually be harder to keep the gorillas safe during the coming off-season, because poachers and local trespassers were more bold when the tourists weren't there. They pointed out some of the places on the mountain where the different families were and where some of the lone males were ranging. Some big showdowns were coming soon, they told me, and some of the lone silverbacks were getting so aggressive that they were almost afraid to track them.

I watched them head off toward the mountain with their rifles, machetes, and notepads to do their afternoon count, and then I went up to the cabin and took a tepid, outdoor shower. I sat on the porch in the sun all afternoon, reading and thinking. I could see cows grazing on some of the deforested hillsides below, but I couldn't see any people. Looking straight west from the high ridge I could see fields and volcanoes and trees upon trees, with hazy blue sky in the forested valley beyond them. I knew that I had traveled through those jungles, and that beyond the trees was the great Congo River and further still, the desert and the ocean.

Sitting there, I felt like all that I'd seen and done, all that I'd been through, was wrapped around me like a cloak, warming me throughout, reshaping me. Watching the sunset over the hills, I felt that I had new skin now, tougher in some places, more permeable in others. And I felt I had new eyes that could see a little better in the dark places, and a little more clearly in the light. As a result of being more patient and more perseverant than I had ever been, of trying to follow my path regardless of the difficulties, I had gained a remarkable feeling of strength and clarity and con-tentment that I had not known before.

When night fell, I went inside and made a small bowl of rice and a cup of tea — the last of the food I had — and sat at the table reading until both of the lanterns burned out and there was only the fire to see by. I opened the door to the woodstove, put on an-other log, and sat in front of it for a long while listening to the noises from the forest and thinking about how I wanted to live and work when I went back home.

When I woke up in the morning, it was still dark, but I was too energized to sleep. I watched the moon drop and sink between the clouds and the mountains, making everything silver before it disappeared. Just as it was gone, the sky began to lighten and as it turned pink, a blue mist formed in the valley. I heated some water and tried to squeeze a cup of tea out of one of the used tea bags. As I was packing up to leave, one of the white-gloved attendants from the lodge came up to invite me to breakfast with the couple from my group. It was Easter Sunday, he said, and they would be pleased to have my company.

I put on my khakis with the legs zipped on, and my best T-shirt and took all my gear with me so that I could leave from there. The manager was annoyed at first by my presence, but when he saw how much fun we were having, he warmed up a bit. The couple, I found out, was on holiday from Saudi Arabia where the man was an executive for a big oil firm. He was from Texas and she was from Holland. We recapped our whole adventure the day before and had omelets and toast and fresh fruit and orange juice and even a little champagne.

Walking down the hill was easier than walking up, but the buses weren't running, so I had to walk twelve miles to the main road. It was a cool, sunny day and the scenery was so beautiful that the pleasure of the walk outweighed the difficulty. I passed a few little farmhouses and a couple of small villages. Kids ran up and pulled at my shirt and reached into my pockets looking for money or treats. One of the villages seemed to be abandoned, but then I heard singing coming from a long, open-air church. The sound was so beautiful that I stopped in the road to listen for a minute. The place was packed and the people were dressed up more than any group of Africans I'd seen. Some of the little girls were even in Easter dresses. As I was walking away, a pretty, smiley teenage girl came out to invite me to the service. "Are you a Jehovah's Witness?" she asked. When I told her that I wasn't, she was very surprised. I think she had been under the impression that all whites were Jehovah's Witnesses. She asked me where I was from and when I told her, she said, "In America, there are many, many Jehovah's Witnesses, yes?"

I told her that yes there were, but not everyone. She seemed sad that I would not come in, but pleased when I told her that I might say some prayers while I was walking. And I did. Instead of walking along grumbling about the lack of rides, I remembered to say a prayer of thanks for all the opportunities I'd had. I thought about how fortunate I was to have made it through Africa in good shape, and how lucky I was to have lived most of my life in a country where it was possible to think about more than just surviving; where logic, reason, technology, and a lot of other things I had often been cynical about, had at least a beneficial foothold. From the far side of Zaire that Easter Sunday, quite a few things looked different to me.

OUT IN THE OPEN

WHEN I FINALLY ARRIVED AT the main road to Goma, I hitched a ride with an Italian prospector who seemed about to lose his mind, and probably his shirt, over a deal gone awry because of government corruption. He wasn't very good company — he didn't even know it was Easter — but I had him deposit me directly at the steps of the Au Rendez-vous, where half of the tourists were still seated as I had left them three days before. I ate a huge dinner and then took a room for the night at the Protestant mission. I was back at the restaurant at eight the next morning for breakfast, and after some souvenir shopping, I was on my way to Rwanda.

The first thing that struck me when I crossed the border into Rwanda was the condition of the roads. Not only were they solid black macadam, but they were edged with ditches and stone guardrails. I hopped on a bus to Kigali that traveled winding, mountainous roads for a couple of hours. The scenery was almost as dramatic as eastern Zaire, alternating between steep, dormant volcanoes and lush farmland, but it was more heavily populated and a little more touched by the influences of modernity. The Italians, I was told, had recently built the roads as part of an eco-nomic aid program, using their experience in the similar terrain of Sicily and Calabria.

In Kigali the people seemed amazingly friendly and unintru-sive. The city was clean and orderly with many modern buildings and plenty of trees and wide avenues. A lot of the locals spoke English as well as French, and I found that for the first time in a long while I could ask for directions or buy something without being worked-over in return. I had read stories about terrible fight-ing in the 1970s between the Hutu and Tutsi populations, fighting that had gotten so vicious at times that one of the rivers running into Burundi to the south had turned red from the blood. Now everything was so orderly and peaceful that such strife seemed in-conceivable. The farming communities seemed to be prosperous. The bustling capital was clean and modern. There was a strong in-frastructure. Here is one African nation, I thought, that has the ability to truly progress and build a great society for its people.

I went to the U.S. embassy to check in and let them know where I was planning to head from there. The sleepy young State Department official behind the counter said he thought I'd prob-ably be happier going north to Uganda or east straight into Tanzania, rather than south to Burundi and then by boat onto Lake Tanganyika. "You could be asking for weeks of delays," he said. "Come back if your plans change."

I told him that I would, but I was surprised when I found myself back there the next morning. The Burundian embassy had simply refused me a visa, without explanation. I asked the official if anyone could intervene on my behalf. He made a few calls within the embassy and came back shaking his head. "Sorry, they do this from time to time," he said. "Apparently they're protesting visa restrictions that we're putting on their own people in Bujumbura. You can try them again tomorrow, but these usually go in two-to three-week cycles."

I couldn't believe that the Burundians wouldn't let me into their country. I walked down the street feeling deflated and trying to rework my plans. On a whim I checked the post office for letters and was surprised to get one from my parents and one from my sister. Apparently they hadn't received any letters all the time I was in Zaire and were very worried that something had happened to me. Their letters were dated two weeks earlier and I knew they must have received some of my letters since then. I wrote a quick page telling them that I was feeling good and that I had made it through the hard places. I told them about the gorillas and the beautiful scenery and about my plans to go see some of the game parks on my way to Nairobi. "I'm almost finished in Africa," I wrote. "Try to enjoy this, the trip is for you also."

I had been thinking all along that the trip would be a fun, vicarious experience for my parents and the rest of the family. I hadn't considered that all of the loneliness that I had felt, and a lot of the hardship was being experienced by them too. The big difference was that whatever I was going through I had some control over, while they had none at all. All they could do was wait for a piece of mail that would tell them what I had been doing a month before.

When I got back to the hostel, I was surprised to see Jan, the Danish drummer who had been with me when I got sick on the truck near Kisangani, checking in at the desk.

"Hey, man. You are alive!" he said, clearly happy to see me. He told me he'd had a terrible time going through the jungle and that Dave, the American, had broken off at Komanda to go into Uganda. Jan had just been to see the gorillas in Rwanda, but it had not been a good experience. "It is shit here," he said. "Don't go. I wish I saw them in Zaire."

I could tell right off that he was starved for company. We put his stuff in my room and then went out for dinner. He told me he was heading straight east to the Serengeti and we decided that we should go together. "I think I'm finished with this jungle scene," he said. "Let's go see some animals out in the open."

In the morning we hopped on a bus to the Tanzanian border and then started hitching east from there. As soon as we got into Tanzania, the roads became dirt again, but they were flat and dusty and easily driveable. It was so arid and sparsely populated that I felt like I was back in West Africa again. Rides were difficult to find and it probably would have seemed like tedious travel again except for the company. Whenever someone tried to overcharge us or when people nagged us, Jan would just make a joke out of it. "Hey man, do you think I am crazy or something?" he would say to them in English. They wouldn't know what he was talking about and neither would I half the time, but we would laugh and the Tanzanians would laugh too.

At night we camped in or near villages along the way, eating the local stews and porridges and looking around as much as we could. In one of the towns we went out into a field to check out the sunset and twenty-five kids followed us to see what we were doing. They wouldn't speak to us, they wouldn't come closer than ten yards, and they wouldn't go away when we told them to. To them we were just strange-looking *mwazungas* with curious clothes and speech patterns. So we decided to have fun with them. When the sun hit the horizon we started bowing and chanting and dancing in circles. The kids backed away and chattered nervously among themselves. Pleased by their reaction, we started yelping and screeching, and by the time the sun disappeared we were on the ground, writhing as if we were having convulsions. Our antics didn't make them any less curious. Some ran away, but they told their friends and by the time we started walking back to town we had a huge crowd. We did our best to entertain them and when we went into a little café for dinner the owner had to go outside and yell at the kids twice before they all dispersed.

We ate millet soup for dinner and drank some coffee, telling stories about life in Denmark and the U.S. When we were walking back to our tent, we heard drums in the distance. "Let's follow them," Jan said, and soon we were wandering down a dark, dirt path on the outskirts of the village. As we got closer we could hear that they were coming from a big party. Eventually we came to a bungalow with people crowded inside and out. We stood on the path for a little while listening to the wild drum beats and watching people. It looked like a college fraternity party except that the women were wearing bright togas made of African cloth.

I didn't think we should go in, but Jan insisted. He had to see the drummers, he said, he had come to Africa primarily for the drumming. I figured we would either be mobbed or resented for crashing the party, but the reaction was neither. A good portion of the town was there, young people and old, and they seemed to welcome our presence. They gave us banana beer and let Jan get on the drums. There were three people drumming at once with no other instruments, and half the people were dancing to the percussive music. I danced too, with a heavy middle-aged woman and a couple of teenage girls who seemed to be daring each other to dance with me. Jan took drum lessons from two of the kids and after a while joined the dancing. "They showed me what they were doing, but I still don't get it," he said with great admiration. "These guys are wild." I can't help but wonder how long afterward the villagers said the same thing about us — the two crazy *mwazungas* who drank banana beer with them and worshiped the sun.

The next day we hitched to the town of Mwanza on Lake Victoria and met one of the many Indian merchants whose family had lived and worked by the lake for generations. "Now they are trying to get us to leave because we are 'foreigners,'" the man told us. "But where can I go? I do not know India. This lake is my home. They say, 'Africa for Africans,' but I am African too." He offered us a ride to Nyalikungu, just to be nice. But I noticed along the way that while he dealt with us as equals and seemed pleased to have our company, he did not seem capable of treating the native Tanzanians the same way.

Soon after he dropped us off, we were heading out of town to find a camping spot, when we saw a pickup truck coming and instinctively held out our thumbs. We were picked up by another local man who offered us a place in the back even though the cab was empty. He was going to drive late, he warned us, because he needed to be in the Serengeti in the morning. Jan and I smiled at each other. "We are having a good day," I said as we hopped into the back of the truck.

The man was a Masai by birth, but his non-African name was Felix and he preferred to go by that. He was a research scientist who worked in parks all over Tanzania. He had gone to college in England and America, and now that he was back in his own country, he found it more backward and disorganized than we did.

"You could have waited a week for a ride there," he said through the window. "You're lucky that I came along."

"We'd only been there twenty minutes," Jan said.

We stopped for dinner in a rustic, buggy café that overlooked Lake Victoria with the sun setting across the water. There was an old ferry heading out across the lake and Felix remarked that the scene had probably looked the same when the British were there in the early part of the century, except that the restaurant would have been better. We toasted the British and watched the boat head off toward Uganda. We had covered more ground in a few days than I had covered in two weeks in Zaire and it felt great.

That night, as we drove along the narrow dirt road in the back of the pickup, we sat and watched the stars above us and the long grassy plains moving by. We thought there might be animals out there, but we were taken completely by surprise when the truck slowed and suddenly there were tall, lumbering shapes moving gracefully beside us. It was a herd of nearly thirty giraffes, some grazing in the trees away from the road, some running not more than fifteen feet away from the truck. They were fast and agile, and there was something surprisingly wild and dangerous about them. Somehow, when they were running, they looked as if they might sprout wings and take off into the sky like great, long-necked dragons. I wanted to stay and watch them all night, but Felix wouldn't stop and he said it would not be safe to leave us there. As we drove on down the straight road, the giraffes shrank slowly until they became part of the dark landscape again. For the rest of the night drive, we kept our eyes peeled and saw zebras, monkeys, ostriches, antelope, and even a few wild buffalo. Each time, they would seem to appear suddenly, and then recede slowly into the night as we watched them.

We slept just outside the Serengeti in the back of the truck while Felix sacked out up front. In the morning, we drove two hours into the park before we came to the rangers' station. There was a campground there, but they wouldn't give Jan and me camping permits because we didn't have a vehicle of our own. "I have been working here for five years and I have never seen any people hitchhiking in the Serengeti," the ranger told us. We were disappointed, but Jan felt it was a great honor too — the first people to hitchhike the Serengeti!

Fortunately Felix hadn't left yet and he agreed to let us tag along with him all the way through the park to the Ngorongoro Crater on its southeastern edge. He was a little annoyed at first and worried about how it looked in front of the rangers, but by the time he finished his errands at the station and we got back on the road, he seemed glad to have us along.

We stopped for lunch on a bluff overlooking a sea of dry grass, with rocky hills on either side in the distance. Felix gave us as much information as we could digest, pointing out different habitat areas and telling us about some of the challenges the different animals were facing. When we complained about not seeing very many inside the park, he told us not to worry. "You'll see plenty of animals up ahead," he said, "and if you don't see them here, you'll see them in the crater." The Ngorongoro Crater was like a natural preserve, he told us, nearly a mile deep and ten miles wide, and the animals had their own ecosystem there. Not even the Masai were allowed to hunt there.

When we asked him to tell us more about the Masai, he was tight-lipped. He said he rarely went back to his village now because he hated dressing up and going through the primitive rituals.

"They honor me because of my great learning," Felix said, "but they do not listen to me when I tell them how to change their ways for the better. Always it is the old ways that rule and I do not agree with many of the old ways."

When Jan asked if he felt lucky to be a Masai, to be part of such a great tradition, he just said no. "I do not even know if I really am a Masai any longer." His goal, he told us, was to go back to England or America and teach at a university. I realized that he was just like some of the travelers I had met. He was unable to integrate what he had seen of the world into his own culture and so he was a man without a country, without a real home.

As we rode along, we could see where it was raining across the plain in spots. Big clouds sat low in the sky and we could just make out the haze of rain below them. All afternoon, we saw the rain clouds moving like gray ships through the sky. Sometimes they were just a half a mile from the truck, curtains of rain falling below them playing wonderful tricks with the light. And sometimes the rain clouds moved right over the road for thirty seconds or a minute, drenching us with warm rain as we rode in the back of the open pickup. And Felix had not lied about the animals. We saw wildebeests and zebras as far as the eye could see in two separate herds of probably ten thousand each. On a bluff near the road there was a lioness yawning and looking out at the zebras. "So many zebras, so little time," I said to Jan. We saw monkeys and ostriches and wild boars and tiny gazelles that could jump fifteen feet while barely moving their legs.

As we climbed up the hill leading out of the park, the sun was going down, and the whole plain spread out below us. We could see tiny dots where some of the animals were, and the orange sun lit up the rain clouds and the surrounding hills. Jan drummed slowly on the bed of the truck, humming quietly to himself.

We passed some Masai herdsmen in traditional red tartan with bald heads, big gold earrings, and long spears. They seemed not to notice us passing, even after we waved to them. Felix barely glanced at them. Soon the crater came into view — an enormous valley surrounded by steep walls with light on one side, shadow on the other. We drove along its edge for a few miles until we got to the park station where Felix was going. We thanked him and wished him luck and then headed further down the road to the campground. As we walked along, the road dipped and curved over little hills. There were very few trees or bushes and we had walked a couple of miles without seeing anyone when a man came along in a Land Rover heading the other way. He was wearing a safari outfit and had a rifle next to him. He surprised us by stopping and looking us up and down.

"Where are you chaps headed?" he asked.

"Up to the campground," I answered, hoping he'd give us a ride.

"Do you have pistols?" he asked, dead serious. When we laughed he said, "People don't usually walk this road without guns, especially at this hour. I wouldn't do it."

"Why is that?" Jan asked.

He looked at us curiously. "Lions," he said, "but you should be okay to the campground. Don't wander at night." He nodded and pulled off.

Jan and I looked at each other. And for the rest of the way we kept our eyes on the bare rises beside us.

"I guess that's why they call it Simba Campground," Jan said as we put up our tents.

There were just a few other tourists at the campground, but they all had jeeps. Until it got dark we could see the rim on the far side of the crater, but we couldn't see the floor of the crater at all. There was no moon and soon we couldn't see more than twenty feet into the surrounding brush. Though we didn't really think there could be much danger, we were both a little jumpy while we cooked and ate our dinner, listening to every little noise beyond the tent. I read for a while and then fell into a deep sleep, only to be wakened by loud growls and heavy steps outside the tent. It sounded like something was sniffing around right at my feet, and then it went away. I stayed perfectly still for fear that any sound might draw attention. But then in the silence when I fell back asleep a loud growl jarred me awake again.

In the morning I was half afraid to open the fly and see what was left of Jan, but when I did, it was a beautiful, sunny day and his tent looked fine.

"Jan, are you awake?" I called.

"Jesus, man. I don't think I slept all night," he said, his voice frayed. He opened his tent. "Did you hear the noises?"

We were sure we'd been stalked by a huge lion, but then we saw hoof prints in the mud all around the camp. We were following them towards the rim when an Australian man camping nearby called to us, "Did ya see that buffalo this mornin'? Dirty bastard, trampled my cookware."

No private vehicles were allowed in the Ngorongoro Park, so like everyone else, we hired a Land Rover with a driver for seventy-five dollars. "Every animal known to East Africa is in the crater," the driver told us before he started us on the tour, "with luck we'll see most of them."

The floor of the crater where they all lived was so deep that we couldn't see any animals at all until we were over halfway down the ridge. Inside, it was a vast green, grassy plain, with two lakes and clumps of trees here and there. A small herd of impala jumped away as we approached. Three elephants eyed us warily, and the driver kept his distance. We watched for a while as two ugly hyenas stalked a small herd of skittish zebras until the hyenas were run off by two male lions who seemed to be protecting the zebras rather than hunting them at the moment.

When we got closer to the biggest lake, I realized that a part of what I thought was shoreline was actually thousands of flamingos standing in the shallow water. And nearby on a small hill was a pride of lions, some not quite fully grown, already started on their midday nap. There were hippos in the deeper water, but they seemed very shy. And there were ten rhinos, each staying alone in its own territory. "If we are very lucky, maybe we will see a white rhinoceros today," the guide said expectantly. And sure enough, just a few minutes later we stumbled upon one who stood and stared back at us the whole time we stared at him.

"This driver is amazing," Jan said mockingly as we rode along with our heads above the big opening in the roof, "I think he may be psychic."

"It's like being at a zoo," I said, "but a pretty good zoo." Across the crater we could see rain clouds forming where we had been a half-hour before. Twenty minutes later it was raining in two different parts of the crater, but it was sunny where we were.

"This place even has its own weather!" Jan yelled above the noise of the engine as we sped along. We saw a few more elephants and some buffalo.

"They are the most dangerous animal in the park," the driver said solemnly, refusing to get close to a large male buffalo that was eyeing us.

"I'll bet that's your friend right there," I said to Jan as the animal began snorting and growling at us. Jan waved a red checkered bandana at him as the driver pulled away towards the road winding back up out of the crater.

We talked about signing up to camp down in the crater or booking a longer safari in the Serengeti, but by the time we got back to the campground we both admitted that we had seen enough animals to hold us for a while. What we really wanted was beds and showers and a good restaurant.

We packed up our tents and hitched our way to the main road at Makuyuni. Three hours later we were boarding a bus to Arusha with fifty Masai. It was market day and they were all dressed in their red and yellow tartan wraps. Most of the women had extensive decorative jewelry, and many of them wore the traditional, wide-bibbed necklaces made of colorful beads. Some of the men were wearing brown or gray sport coats with their wraps, and a few of them were carrying their long spears. Everybody was very bald and wonderfully friendly.

"I love this," Jan kept saying. "This is my idea of a good day!"

And it got even better, in a way. When we got to Arusha, we had been talking about staying a few days and maybe trying to climb Kilimanjaro. But we couldn't see the mountain because of clouds, and the town was so disappointing that we didn't want to stay. We hitched another ride to the Kenyan border and the next thing we knew, we were on a bus to Nairobi. By nine o'clock we were in an Australian bar in downtown Nairobi eating pizza, drinking beer, and celebrating our successful crossing of the continent.

FLYING AWAY

JAN AND I FIGURED we would go out again from Nairobi on a proper safari or to climb Mount Kenya or Kilimanjaro. I intended all along to really explore the parks in Kenya and Tanzania, and to travel to the coast for a good week to rejuvenate before heading on to India. But once I got in the city, it pulled me in and didn't let go.

For a week we ate four meals a day and went to a movie almost every night. We went out drinking with a couple of Australian women we met at the hostel and I spent long hours in the American Cultural Center reading not only back issues of the *International Herald Tribune*, but all kinds of magazines from the States — *Newsweek, People, American Cinematographer, Sports Illustrated*. Some of the movies I had worked on the previous year had come out and one of them had received some Academy

Award nominations. My college football team had had a good season. The Redskins had done poorly. The stock market had done so well that when I added up the few stocks I had, the increases almost exactly matched the amount I'd spent traveling in Africa.

I went to the American Express office twice a day and picked up three letters from my grandparents, two from my Aunt Winnie, four from friends, a few from my brothers, sister, and cousins, and five from my parents. I pored over all the news and tried to fill in between the lines and imagine all the details of the months I had missed. My youngest brother had been accepted to a college in Florida. My sister had started dating someone from work who was "wonderful and funny" and unlike anyone she had dated before. My parents gave me tidbits of news from each of the weeks they wrote, but mostly, they said, they were sad from missing me and exhausted from worrying about where I was and how I was doing. "You should see your poor father," my mother wrote in one letter, "his hair has turned gray during the past two months." They had finally gotten most of my letters, but apparently I had made a mistake in telling too many details about cutting my foot on the boat and getting sick near Kisangani. What seemed to me like pretty normal afflictions in Africa had sounded horrible to my family so far away.

I booked a ticket to Bombay on Pakistan Airways for two hundred dollars — including an expense-paid, thirty-hour layover in Karachi. It took me three days to get my visa for India and make other preparations, including getting my beat up "congo boots" resoled. By the time Jan was ready to head out to the coast, I didn't have enough time to go with him. I walked to the Nairobi train station with him and the two Australian women and saw them off to Mombasa.

"There are trains in India," Jan yelled from the window as they pulled out. "Trains!"

I wandered the streets feeling alone and harried as person after person asked for money. I went to the American Express office to check for new mail, but there was none. I decided that I should call home at the telephone-telegraph office to tell everyone about my plans. After waiting forty-five minutes to get an international line, I got my parent's answering machine and was cut off midsentence after I had given the flight numbers and dates and a few of the cities to send mail to in India. When they said it would be another forty-five minute wait to call again, I let it go. At least now they knew where I was going and that I was safe and sound. I walked down the street to a big movie theater and watched a Spielberg film about British POWs in China during World War II. By the time I left the theater, all my thoughts were on India and China.

I got a haircut the next day, my first since New York, and then I made a pilgrimage to the Isak Dinesen homestead. I had to change buses three times and walk a mile to get there, but it was worth it. The area nearby had obviously grown since she left in the thirties. There were stores and a busy intersection nearby, but her home was still peaceful, with a panorama green and tan hills spread out beyond the backyard. I sat on the lawn and read for the afternoon and then wandered through the house, wondering how it might have been when she was there. I tried to imagine the music and the conversation and the solitude.

Isak Dinesen, I knew, had seen much in the hardship and dignity of Africa. It had inspired her and defined her and in many ways freed her. She found sanctuary in its rugged beauty and it never loosened its hold on her once she left.

Has Africa done the same to me, I wondered, as I sat looking out at the Ngong Hills? Has it changed me? Will it stay with me? I had been on the road for nearly six months — four months in Africa. Though I had longed to immerse myself in a world without the complications of modernity, I'd had no concept of what such a world would actually be like. Even though I had read about the sandy vegetables and rancid meat, the crowded trucks, the mud holes, the corrupt soldiers, the long sunsets, and the melodic songs, there was no possibility of truly conceiving it without having seen it.

I had wanted to be alone for a while, but I had not expected loneliness that was almost physically painful. I had wanted to experience new and different worlds, but I had not expected to learn what it was like to be marked as an outsider day after day, to feel at times desperate for something familiar to hold on to. I had wanted to meet some interesting people along the way, but I had not expected to find smiles and voices and brief friendships that would stand in my mind forever. Most of all, I had wanted to find art and expand my aesthetic sensibilities, but I had not expected to be touched by Africa's quiet suffering as much as by its beauty.

Looking back, I realized that I was lucky to be able to walk alone through the jungle, and sit alone on the shore of the Niger River, and camp alone in the dunes of the Sahara. The hard conditions had tested me again and again, stripping me down, pushing me beyond my limits, beyond myself. And the beauty and quietude of the people and the landscapes had fed me and uplifted me, replenishing my emotional reservoirs and filling my loneliness. In the end, I had found something that I hadn't known I was looking for. I had wanted to learn new things about the world, but I had learned as much about myself as anything else. I had learned what it was like to walk alone through the world. Having crossed through Africa alone, I knew that I could survive almost anything, that I could stand on my own and trust myself in any situation. Africa had given me much more than its colors and rhythms, its peaceful smiles and languid sunsets. It had given me a sense of reality and clarity about myself and the world around me.

I woke up on April 15, 1989, in a windowless room at a Nairobi hostel feeling nervous and worried about my evening flight to Pakistan. I had bought a travel guide to India, but nothing for Pakistan and I really had little idea what to expect in either country. I knew there would be good food and trains and a lot more tourists to rub elbows with, but I didn't know much else. I still didn't have a concrete plan for where to go once I got there or how to move from India toward home (though someone had told me about a way to travel overland through China by crossing the Himalayas in northern Pakistan and then heading east). If I could find a way, I wanted to go to Tibet and spend some time at a monastary, but from what the embassy had told me, the Chinese government allowed only official tour groups in the Tibetan region.

After packing and repacking my bags, I went shopping for souvenirs in the Nairobi market and then had a late lunch with an elderly British couple I met at the American Express office. They had booked two photo safaris and one birding cruise for their three-week vacation. They were surprised by how rustic Nairobi was and how many sick and poverty-stricken people there were on the streets. Their safari agency had promised good vehicles, fine food, and comfortable accommodations, but after seeing their hotel, they weren't sure what they had gotten themselves into. "Don't worry," I told them. "You'll have a great time. Just close your eyes, take a deep breath, and take everything unusual as part of the adventure. You won't even notice the dirt after a while."

"I suppose that's the difference between a traveler and a tourist," the woman said, smiling.

"Perhaps it is," I replied. "That, and the condition of their shoes." They both leaned over and took a look at my thin African sandals. The new scars on my foot and heel showed next to the dark leather. The resoled "congo boots" were in my bag.

As I rode the bus out to the airport late that afternoon, I watched my last views of Africa roll by. People were pushing heavy carts down the dirt sidewalks and kids played soccer in dusty lots. Here and there, women were tending gardens and sometimes the vista would open up to a grassy field with a lone cow grazing and wide-topped trees marking the horizon.

Africa is an isolated continent, I thought, remembering similar scenes in every country I had traveled through. It seemed strange that even in Nairobi there could be the feeling of isolation and neglect — by the local government and by the rest of the world. Often I had felt the tragedy of that isolation, the debilitating barriers it created, the sad loss of potential. But I knew that the natural serenity which made Africa so unique was rooted in its isolation as well. The modern world was slowly finding its way into the continent, for good and bad. I knew that if I ever came back it would undoubtedly be a very different place.

I sat in the airport with the Arabs, Hindus, and Africans, glad to be moving on and sad to be leaving a place that had in many ways come to feel like home. I watched the ebony-skinned baggage handlers loading suitcases onto the Pakistan Airways jet and then I boarded the plane, handing my ticket to a female flight attendant who wore a green scarf draped under her chin from ear to ear.

As the plane took off, I watched the trees, buildings, dirt roads, highways, fields, and floodlights slowly shrink below me and disappear. And I was left alone with the stars above the Indian Ocean and the memories of a rough, quiet continent that inevitably touches the heart of anyone who travels in it.

AFTERWORD

AFRICA HAS CHANGED a great deal since I traveled there in the late 1980s. Many of the routes I took then have been closed off by turmoil, reopened, and closed again. Most of the countries I passed through have changed governments and many have adopted new constitutions, sometimes amidst terrible upheaval.

In Algeria, fundamentalists have attempted to assert their claim to the national government and the country has been wracked by political violence with tens of thousands of innocent people killed. The unrest in Algeria, combined with the travel restrictions in Libya and the continuing turmoil along the Egypt-Sudan route, make the Sahara more hazardous and less open to travel today than perhaps at any time since World War II.

In sub-Saharan Africa, the situation has not been much better, and in some cases it has been even worse. Niger adopted a constitution, but the new president was ousted in a military coup. Ten years of low rainfall has reduced livestock herds to a tenth of their former levels and the end of the cold war has meant decreasing revenues from the uranium mines in the north. Niger remains a poor country poised on the edge of progress if the rains come, and on the edge of disaster if they do not.

After student protests led to the ouster of its longtime president, Mali does seem to be edging toward progress. In subsequent elections, an opposition party candidate won, making Mali the third African nation (after Benin and Zambia) to make a peaceful transition from a one-party to a multi-party system. A similar multi-party system was adopted in the Ivory Coast in 1990, but the ruling party there has maintained power. As the Ivory Coast continues to expand its relatively vibrant economy, there is hope among intellectuals that civil society will prevail in coming years and the country can become a model for West African democracy as well.

Elsewhere in former French Africa the picture is not as hopeful. After France pulled out its troops and swore off future interventions in 1996, the Central African Republic was blacklisted by the International Monetary Fund. The C.A.R. continues to struggle economically, and is under pressure from both internal upheavals and troubles in bordering states.

Nowhere in Africa has the political turmoil and loss of life been greater than in Rwanda and Zaire, where both governments have fallen in violent civil wars. Rwanda has been torn apart by ethnic warfare and acts of inhumanity that are beyond comprehension — with more than 1.5 million people slaughtered and equal numbers uprooted and driven out of the country into refugee camps in Tanzania and Zaire. In both Rwanda and Burundi to the south, fighting between the Hutus and the Tutsis continues to flare up, and it seems that it will be a long time before these deep ethnic wounds can be healed. Surprisingly, the mountain gorillas of the Ruwenzori range have been affected very little by the turmoil in the valleys

below them. Though many hillsides have been stripped for firewood
and food by refugees, the gorillas and their habitat have been largely
left alone.

In Zaire, it was the inability of President Mobutu Sese Seko to
control the Rwandan refugee camps that signaled Laurent Kabila
to begin a rebellion that swept across that country. As Kabila's
Tutsi-aided forces marched toward the capital, tens of thousands
of Rwandan Hutu refugees were slaughtered in their path, along
with international aid workers and many Zairians. After taking
power, Kabila changed Zaire's name back to the Democratic
Republic of the Congo and promised free elections, but not until
1999, after he has "established order" in the country. His government has been promised U.S. aid, but continues to defy United
Nations efforts to investigate the mass killing of refugees.

And in Kenya, once the shining star of post-colonial Africa,
the government has devolved into one of the most embarrassingly
regressive regimes on the continent. After being pressured into
accepting multi-party reforms, longtime president Daniel Arap-
Moi has worked to divide the opposition by systematically ex-
ploiting tribal differences, curtailing civil rights, and plundering
the treasury for his own party's use. Moi was recently re-elected to
a final five-year term in an election that was widely criticized by
international observers. Increasingly, foreign tourists are heading
to the game parks of South Africa and Botswana to see animals
that were once synonymous with the name Kenya.

Travel in Africa today continues to require measures of cau-
tion, empathy, and perseverance. AIDS, malaria, dysentery, and
other epidemics have ravaged local populations over the past
decade. Nearly half of the people on the continent are still living
on the equivalent of less than one dollar a day. Economic change
might be accelerating as a new generation of leaders begins to take
power, but a traveler on the rural roads or in the small towns would
likely find today pretty much what I found then — a quiet people
who simply want to live their lives without being oppressed by

poverty or politics. Some of the scenes depicted in this book will probably be recognizable to a visitor 150 years from now. Others had doubtless changed even before I left the continent. It is easy for most of us to ignore such a faraway place burdened with so many endemic problems, but once encountered firsthand, Africa is impossible to forget.

Kevin Kertscher
February, 1998

ACKNOWLEDGMENTS

This book would not have been written without the encouragement and support of two people: my father, who kept saying "come home" the whole time I was traveling and then started lobbying for a written account of the trip as soon as I got back; and my writing teacher, Barbara Kreiger, whose passion for travel literature inspired me, and whose patience, confidence, and ideas guided me from beginning to end.

Thanks to my other Dartmouth readers, especially Noel Perrin who gave many good ideas for improving the text, and to the writing gang, Rebecca Armstrong, Teresa Lust, Carol Ehlen, Alicia Green, Joan Kersey, Mark Laser, Maggie Montgomery, and Katherine Niemela, who read through early chapters with good humor and helped me shape my ideas. Thanks also to those who gave thoughtful readings on later drafts, including Kathryn and

Tory Teague, Barbara and Sarah Fraunfelder, Amy Meeker, Camilla Rockwell, Mark Purushotham, and the eagle-eyed Rina Bander.

"Merci" to Amy Sachrison and David Borde who helped me with the French, and "shokran" to the snack vendor at the JFK/UMASS subway stop who smiled patiently when I accidently interrupted his prayers, and then helped me with Arabic spellings when he finished.

I especially appreciate the confidence and advice of my editor, Alan Lelchuk, and the hard work of the Steerforth staff who patiently tolerated my inexperience — Robin Dutcher-Bayer, Tim Jones, Chip Fleischer, and Helga Schmidt.

Most of all, my thanks and love to my mom, Nancy Kertscher, who has been more excited about the book as it has come together than anyone else, and to Kate Fraunfelder, who helped keep me writing in France, Italy, Cape Cod, and Boston.

I would never have ventured into the Sahara if Joe Ruzecki hadn't dreamed up the idea, or set off around the world by myself if my usual travel partner, Ian McKenna, hadn't kept me awake so many camping nights musing over the possibilities. I wish they could have come with me. And I would never have completed the trip without the help of the many people who opened their homes, fed me, and gave me rides and advice along the way, especially the Peace Corps volunteers and the aid workers who make it a full time job to help anyone who needs them.